Sh

ift

A Marketing Rethink

Published by:

PHD

Bankside 2,
90-100 Southwark Street,
London, SE1 0SW, UK

www.phdmedia.com

For more content, including videos of the interviews in this book, visit www.shiftbyphd.com

Lead Author:

Mark Holden

Consultant Author:

Jeremy Lee

Co-authors:

Andrew Mclean

Anthony Koziarski

Ben Hovanooo

Charli Ursell

Chris Stephenson

James Buckle

Kate King

Michael Florence

Rohan Tambyrajah

Contributors:

Alex Newman

Avin Narasimhan

Desmond Bateman

Gemma Spence

Louise Johnson

Malcolm Devoy

Matt McNeany

Matt Prentis

Miranda Bird

Paul Cuckoo

Phillip Rees

Scott Hagedorn

Shona Read

Slavi Samardzija

Tom Darlington

Tom Mackenzie

Ceri Ellis – Specialist Teacher in Learning Differences

Justin Bell – Credera

Mark Ritson – The Mini MBA in Marketing

Sally Dominguez – Singularity University

Interviewees:

Andrew Robertson – BBDO

Anna Suchopar – ASOS

Bruce Daisley – Author

Byron Sharp – Ehrenberg Bass Institute for Marketing Science

Conny Braams – Unilever

Daryl Simm – OMG

Dave Trott – Copywriter and Author

David Indo – ID Comms

Debasree Dasgupta – Pepsi

Gerhard Louw – Lindt & Sprüngli

Henrik Wenders – Audi

Ian Mundorff – HP

Isabel Massey – Diageo

Jeffrey F. Rayport – Harvard Business School

Katie Best – Katie Best Associates & Head Tutor at LSE

Les Binet – adam&eveDDB

Nancy F. Koehn – Harvard Business School

Patricia Corsi – Bayer

Polly Cochrane – WarnerMedia

Richard Shotton – Astroten

Siobhan Randall – Multiverse

Stefan Buescher – Volkswagen Group

Suresh Balaji – HSBC

Special thanks to:

Amanda Salerno

Avril Canavan

Jessica Ozdemir

Marjan Mohsenin – Singularity University

Melissa Brookes – In the Margin

Print:

BlackDog Digital

Cover Design:

Wayne Ford

Design:

BlackDog Studio

Illustrations:

Paul Price

Fore

word

From Philippa Brown.
Chief Executive Officer, PHD Worldwide.

After what has been one of the most challenging years in many of our lives, we are delighted to launch our latest book, *Shift, A Marketing Rethink*.

Thought leadership is at the heart of PHD's DNA. Our vision is to be the most creative and strategic agency in a data and tech world. One of the ways we support this vision is through the creation of our thought-pieces and books. We have built a library of 10 books over 10 years covering subjects such as gamification, emerging technology and challenger thinking. Each of these books has been written with a sole focus of empowering our people to help their clients make a leap (PHD's positioning) in terms of creativity and therefore business growth.

This latest book, ***Shift***, sets out to help marketers and agencies rethink the way that they structure their marketing. It starts with a reflection on the past decade, and the changes that have taken place, and then looks forward to how we can reorganize and rebuild for the future.

It is a practical and easily digestible book and has been written to enable you to pick up and put down, to fit in with your busy schedules. Hopefully it is a perfect companion for when we get back to traveling again.

I would like to personally thank everyone who contributed to this book. My special thanks go to Mark Holden—PHD's Worldwide Chief Strategy Officer—who has worked tirelessly on writing and producing this book.

I really hope you enjoy reading it and if you have any comments or thoughts you would like to share, feel free to email me directly at *philippa.brown@phdmedia.com*

Con

tents

Intro duc tion

Life used to be a lot simpler. Particularly if you work in marketing.

That is because the continual advancements in data and technology, along with the impact of COVID-19, have radically *reorganized* the practice of marketing.

As you are no doubt aware, the dramatic increase in the number and type of touchpoints, the explosion of digital-commerce and the maturation of data and marketing technologies, has resulted in a remarkably rich tapestry from which to build marketing strategies.

The result, of course, is that there is an almost unlimited combination of activities that could be deployed when planning a marketing campaign. And therein lies the problem: complexity.

Increasing complexity leads to an *increasing* need for consultancy.

With this diverse and multi-dimensional canvas comes an increasing need for expertise to guide marketing. Whereas 10 to 20 years ago marketers, broadly, knew what they needed their agencies to execute prior to briefing them, now they are less sure. Or there is a sense that the current approach may not be optimal.

Therefore, the requirement for an agency is less about the transactional and more on the advisory, which is causing significant growing pains for agencies. Today, the agency has to cover a much wider footprint of expertise—some of which is not an evolution of the current scope, instead bringing in new capabilities that the leadership may not be familiar with. For example, many leaders of media agencies are leading businesses that are much more advanced and, in some cases, unrecognizable from the businesses where they spent the first part of their careers.

Barriers to evolution.

Added to that, agencies are trying to find a balance between what their clients need—full-spectrum marketing support—and what their clients are, typically, willing to pay for: a legacy payment model that, for the media agencies, is often referenced back to a percentage of media spend, and therefore still anchored in transaction.

Agencies can only develop their product offering *with* their clients, as the need for building advanced capabilities ahead of revenue is a challenge for most businesses. The two main barriers to development are either a lack of foresight on the agency side—on how their product offering needs to evolve—or a lack of willingness for clients to invest in these new areas. If either of these conditions exist, they serve as an immediate showstopper to evolution.

Some 'client-side' marketing organizations have instead looked to build the capability within. There have been some success stories, and some have reversed the decision. Finding talent has not proven to be the challenge; it is retaining, developing and, ultimately, easily replacing the talent that is the real challenge. Other, unexpected, issues popped up such as how to manage the billing process with media vendors and tech companies. We explore this further in Chapter 3.

Even where there is a logical basis for the in-housing of certain capabilities, the marketing organization needs the support of the agencies—whether in the form of talent, data, technology, third-party relationships, preferable contracts or curated inventory services.

For those agencies that have lost some functions to their clients, many have built new capabilities and, therefore, revenues. What is clear is that the nature of the agency is changing, dramatically. Agencies just need to think clearly about their customers—what they want, of course, but more importantly, what they need.

Reconfiguring the agency around the marketing organization.

It is becoming clear that it is time to rethink the agency. This is particularly the case for the media agency, which needs to fully evolve its product offering from just media services, to that of a true *marketing* agency.

And for all agencies to be more modular in nature. To offer a range of support functions that can be compiled, bespoke for a client, and wrapped around them. With agency leadership that can provision and support in-sourced talent into their clients' organizations, whilst connecting them to out-sourced talent within the agency. *Hubbing* advanced services, in cities where the talent is more readily available, and *off-shoring* more commoditized services. Putting in place processes to remove workflow inefficiencies, with technology that removes friction; that also removes the gaps between client and agency, global and local and creative and media. And leads to a simple connected workflow—bringing in each specialist at the right moment.

However, as important as data and technology is, the emphasis has to be brought back to the individual talent. In the way that data and technology were the focus for the last decade, the management of talent needs to be the focus for the next decade. This is something we explore more fully in Chapter 4.

Building this new model is a psychological task as much as it is an engineering task. It is a fascinating area for exploration. Thinking about the new types of talent that need to be brought into the business for the future is something we explore in the final chapter. And arguably, as marketing departments and agencies reach a point of parity in the race for data and technology advancement, it is the next area for development■

And this is the focus for *Shift*■

In this new post-COVID world, *Shift* takes stock of where we are and where we could be heading. Taking a look back at the wave of complexity that built up over the last decade with the resultant midlife crises it has caused in marketing. And looking ahead, how marketing appears to be changing, the implications for talent and the new functions that are likely to emerge over the next five to 10 years.

And how these new, and existing, functions best click-together in a connected, healthy and functioning ecosystem, where the boundaries between marketing organization and agency disappear.

The ambition for this book is to be more than the opinion of one person or group. Instead, it casts the net wide to bring together the opinion of many of the leaders in marketing, across a range of organizations and practices, and attempts to crystallize the consistent themes. This is supported by newly-commissioned research into the views of marketers on the future of marketing.

As much as possible, it has been written to be a practical guide for marketers and their agencies—with mini summaries, tips and suggested workshops. We really hope it adds to the thinking, and debate, you are having in your own organization. Anyway, that's the ambition.

Let's now get into it.

As it's time to make the

Sh

ift

Chapter 1:

That Wave of

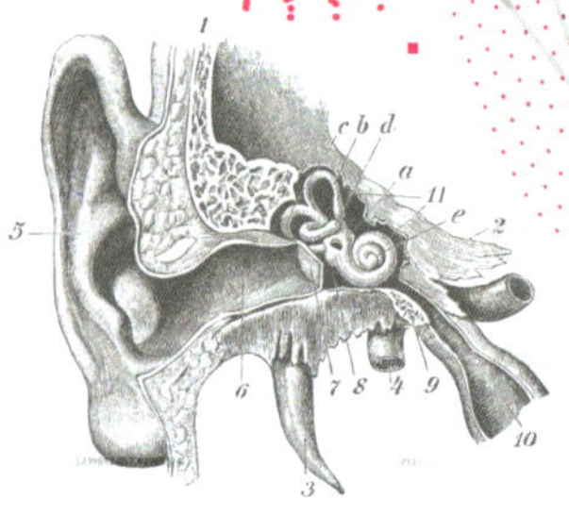

01

Complexity

The marketing industry has always experienced change. But the changes it experienced over the 13-year period between 2007 and 2020 were unprecedented. We are going to call this 13-year period the 'long decade'.

The primary driver of these changes was, of course, technological advancement. Patterns of media consumption went through their most rapid shifts in decades—to new environments on new types of devices. And we witnessed remarkable changes to the practice of marketing. This chapter covers the major events that led to the levels of complexity we face today.

This shift did not appear out of nowhere. In order to sequence the events that took place we are going to use that classic business book technique of invoking a parallel to something completely unrelated. Namely the prehistoric period called the Cambrian explosion. The Cambrian explosion, as of course you are aware, was a period in history where dramatic changes happened to the earth's environment which led to the development of complex life. Before that period, life forms on earth were so simple that key features of modern-day organisms like ears, eyes and gills did not yet exist. But afterwards, there was an explosion of variety and complexity.

We think this is an effective, albeit marginally pretentious, metaphor for the long decade—a period of dramatic change that resulted in the *birth* of a new marketing and media infrastructure within which we all operate.

The Cambrian explosion of media

One can think of the Cambrian explosion in media as unfolding in three key stages:

Before: The foundational elements that were in place before the change

During: The environmental shifts that created the explosion

After: The new media features that came into existence

Let's look at these three stages and the resultant impact on marketing.

Before: The foundational elements that were in place before the change

The internet

The internet was widely available in most consumer markets by 2007, but primarily as a landline service piped to homes and businesses. Mobile internet connectivity was slow or impractical beyond Wi-Fi use cases. But the internet was nearly 30 years old at this point in history, so the core infrastructure was well-developed, and consumers were familiar with various applications. The dotcom boom was about seven years in the past, and Google had gone public in 2004. But internet devices, at this time, were primarily desktop and laptop computers—limiting consumption of internet-delivered content and services.

eCommerce

Retailers had been using the internet as a sales channel since the 1990s, and the world's most famous and successful eCommerce businesses—Amazon and Alibaba—were both founded in that decade. But in 2007, eCommerce was a relatively small fraction of retail sales, comprising only three to 10 percent of total retail volume in major markets.

Cell phones

In 2007, cell phones were a 30-year-old technology and had achieved significant penetration into most consumer markets. More than three billion devices were in use around the world. These devices were not particularly capable, with weak processors, low-resolution (and non-touch) displays, and slow connectivity, but they were widely adopted because of the core talk and text utility they provided. Primitive smartphones like the Nokia Communicator and Palm Treo existed but had a limited audience due to various shortcomings.

Social media

Social media platforms like Facebook and Twitter were around in 2007 and were growing in popularity, but they had yet to achieve the success they would later attain. Facebook and Twitter were both using feed-based environments—a primary viewing portal characterized by an endlessly scrolling feed of content, but usage and penetration were relatively low as people could not access these platforms on-the-go. That meant their nascent ad offerings lacked scale, limiting their appeal to advertisers.

Ad auctions in limited use

The practice of using advertiser bids to set ad prices had been invented but were not in wide use in 2007. While ad auctions had first been commercialized by Overture in 1998, it was not until 2002 that Google implemented them at scale. Ad auctions were regarded as a curiosity by the ad industry at large, which continued to rely on rate-cards to set prices for the vast majority of advertising. Marketers viewed auctions warily, as they leveled the playing field by denying large advertisers the rate advantages they were accustomed to in traditional media.■

During: The environmental shifts that created the explosion.

In 2007, the addition of three catalyzing shifts kicked off the incredible rate of change in digital media:

Faster networks

The development of faster networks, both fixed-line and mobile, took off in 2007. Networks moved from 2G to 3G and then to 4G, with 5G mobile networks now being gradually rolled out. Average mobile connection speeds increased tenfold in a handful of years, rapidly scaling from 1Mbps to 10Mbps to 100Mbps and now to 1000Mbps in key markets.

Simultaneously, there has been an enormous build-out of fixed-line infrastructure in most countries, ranging from fiber-to-the-home to improvements to existing cable infrastructure. This pushed typical home internet speeds in the developed world from 10Mbps in 2007 to 100Mbps today—far above the threshold of about 20Mbps needed to stream the highest-quality 4K video. In parallel, the Wi-Fi networks in peoples' homes got dramatically faster during the long decade so that Wi-Fi no longer bottlenecks fast internet connections.

Taken as a whole, these advancements enabled a new class of rich media experiences for wirelessly connected internet devices.

Advances in computing power

Before the long decade, there was a truism in computer processors: high performance required lots of electrical power. A mobile processor using lots of power would therefore demand not only a capacious battery, but also elaborate cooling solutions like large fans and heatsinks to dissipate the resulting waste heat. No one is going to be stuffing such a cooling solution into a device as small as a phone or a streaming stick.

This truism—that it was impossible to combine high performance and low power consumption—finally broke during the long decade. It became possible for the first time to create a processor that could meet both performance and power criteria at once. This was enabled by the combination of a new chip design (ARM) optimized for energy efficiency. As the production of these processors scaled, their costs collapsed, driving down the cost of computing power across various classes of devices.

Better, cheaper displays

Before the long decade, flat panel displays of all types and specialized displays, like the high-resolution capacitive (not requiring a stylus) touchscreens that are ubiquitous today in smartphones and tablets, were wildly expensive. Over the long decade that changed dramatically. Enormous capital investments by the largest display producers like LG and Samsung, as well as competition from China, hammered the price down so even the highest-quality touchscreen displays could be obtained for a relative pittance. The large panel sizes we now take for granted in the TV market followed a similar price trajectory. Cheap displays meant cheaper devices, in the hands of more consumers.

The confluence of these three enabling technologies—faster networks, advances in computing power, and better, cheaper displays—resulted in the emergence of two major families of hardware to proliferate: smartphones (including tablets) and connected TVs. Both significantly contributed to the Cambrian explosion. See boxes.

Smartphones and tablets

Apple was the first to successfully integrate fast-enough networking, a fast but low-power processor and a highly responsive capacitive touchscreen into a mobile device. The result was the iPhone (2007 onwards), the most successful single product in business history. Competitors quickly followed suit, leading to a wide variety of Android devices from a huge number of manufacturers.

The extraordinary success of the smartphone device category has seen it go from being a rounding error in the overall mobile phone industry, with just 64 million sold in 2006, to being the dominant computing devices on the planet, with more than 3.5 billion smartphones estimated to be in use in 2020 against a world population of 7.8 billion adults. Smartphones today account for an enormous share of media time consumption, with adults in the US spending three hours per day, or 25 percent of their media time, with these devices.▪

Connected TVs

The same technological tailwinds that saw smartphones gain widespread popularity drove a shift in the very nature of televisions. Smart TVs had been a dream for decades—at least since the 1990s when experiments like WebTV were brought to market—but had never gained traction. During the long decade, the combination of cheap low-power processors, fast networks, inexpensive large flat-panel displays, and the rollout of digital TV transmission meant that for the first time, TV manufacturers could add intelligence and support for IP-based video to their TVs at very little extra cost.

Smart TVs went from being a niche product to the default offering, scaling from one percent penetration in the US in 2010 to 58 percent penetration in 10 years. For those consumers who did not wish to upgrade to these new smart TVs with built-in apps and internet connectivity, a variety of manufacturers like Roku filled the gap with inexpensive streaming sticks. These sticks enabled IP streaming video delivery to TVs for as little as $20 to $30. As a practical matter, cost was no longer a barrier to getting IP-delivered video onto a TV screen.

With these two classes of devices in billions of hands and households, practically every consumer in the world had the means to access rich IP-delivered content both at home and on the go.■

The stage was set for a Cambrian explosion of new media features. A whole range of these emerged and can be clustered into the following five groups:

After: The new media features that came into existence.

1

Social: Huge scaling of social media

From 2007 to 2020, social media usage exploded worldwide as smartphone adoption skyrocketed, leading to the advent of newsfeeds, promoted posts and stories. Existing networks like Facebook and Twitter prospered, and new platforms like Instagram, Snap, Pinterest and TikTok were all brought to market. We now measure the largest platforms in terms of billions, or hundreds of millions, of monthly active users. Social media time increased by more than 100 percent between 2007 and 2020. That made their ad offerings extremely powerful vehicles not just for driving reach, but also for driving performance outcomes through their sophisticated ads delivery optimization capabilities. Advertisers had the opportunity to start to think about these platforms holistically as part of an end-to-end solution, rather than viewing them as a point solution for *reach* or *performance*.

2 *Data: Ubiquitous data collection of user activity to drive and measure ad performance*

The movement of consumer activity onto the internet enabled vast systems of data collection and tracking, which were of enormous benefit to advertisers. Ad delivery systems created by platforms like Facebook, Google and Alibaba harness an enormous array of signals to optimize ad serving, so a given ad is served to users most likely to engage with it, resulting in the birth of first-, second- and third-party data sets. Within this came the advent of behavioral-data, based on actual online actions. This offered an enormous improvement to the efficiency of advertising delivery. The dark side, however, is that ever-more personal data about consumers was being captured by large corporations. That has spawned a regulatory response from governments, with GDPR in the European Union and the CCPA in the US and with more regulation almost certain to follow.

3 *Streaming: Streaming displacing traditional broadcast/cable/satellite TV/gaming*

The proliferation of fast networks and fast processors made it possible to deliver high quality video over the internet at an unprecedented scale. Fast networks meant that video bit-rates (the amount of raw data per second of video) could increase. And fast processors meant that computers of all kinds were more capable than ever of decoding complex video compression schemes, which meant that a video stream could deliver high quality at low bit rates. People could stream high-quality video to mobile devices as well as their living room TV for the first time at a low cost. The result was a fragmentation in the supply of video ads and the introduction of new features such as skippable formats and dynamic versioning, for each individual. In 2020, with a massive installed base, traditional TV providers saw their subscriber numbers and market share fall in the face of this competition. That meant marketers had to completely re-evaluate their video advertising approach as we headed into the next decade. Faster networks also fueled web-enabled gaming across various consoles and PCs. And with this, video streaming of other people playing—leading to a sudden rise of new platforms such as Twitch, a live-streaming video service.

---

4 *eCommerce: Online sales become a major part of retail*

The mass popularity of smartphones gave eCommerce businesses the opportunity to scale beyond traditional PCs. With powerful mobile devices in the hands of billions, eCommerce was able to grow to a substantial portion of overall retail sales. Even more interesting is how the growth of eCommerce varied across markets. In developed countries like the US and UK, eCommerce growth continued roughly the same trajectory it was on prior to the long decade. But in China, the combination of smartphones and WeChat led to explosive eCommerce growth: at the end of the long decade eCommerce was approximately 50 percent of all retail sales. The shift to eCommerce meant marketers had to take a much more dynamic approach to advertising.

5 *Ad Auctions: Scaling bid-based trading models as the primary method of selling inventory*

Auction-based advertising requires media to be IP-based, as there is a two-way stream of data between the advertiser's systems and the consumer's device. Therefore, as more activity moved onto the internet, from reading the news to watching TV and movies to shopping, the advertising supporting these media forms became compatible with auction-based advertising. This led to an explosion of auction-based advertising across all digital media forms, steadily displacing traditional rate-card based buying. That meant advertisers had to pay more attention than ever to their ad costs, and increasingly consider their bid strategy as a core part of their media buying efforts. The move to an auction model also lowered barriers to entry for advertisers, enabling small and mid-sized businesses to access major ad markets for the first time and diminished the scale advantages for large advertisers. Whole categories were disrupted in the process.

The Cambrian explosion of media.

New features that came into existence after 2007 (or at least matured into the product we experience today)

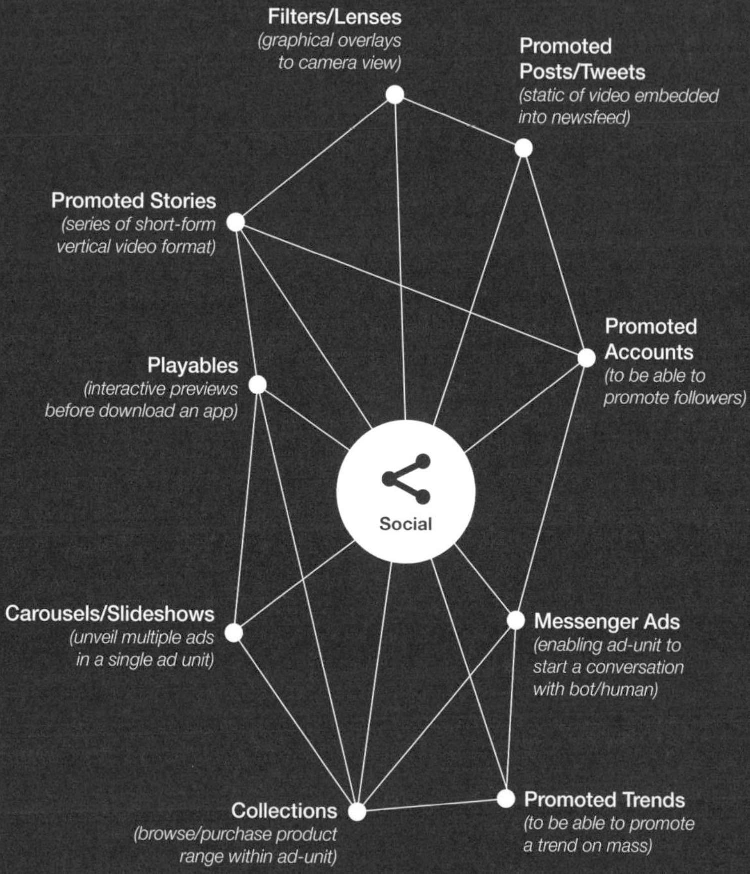

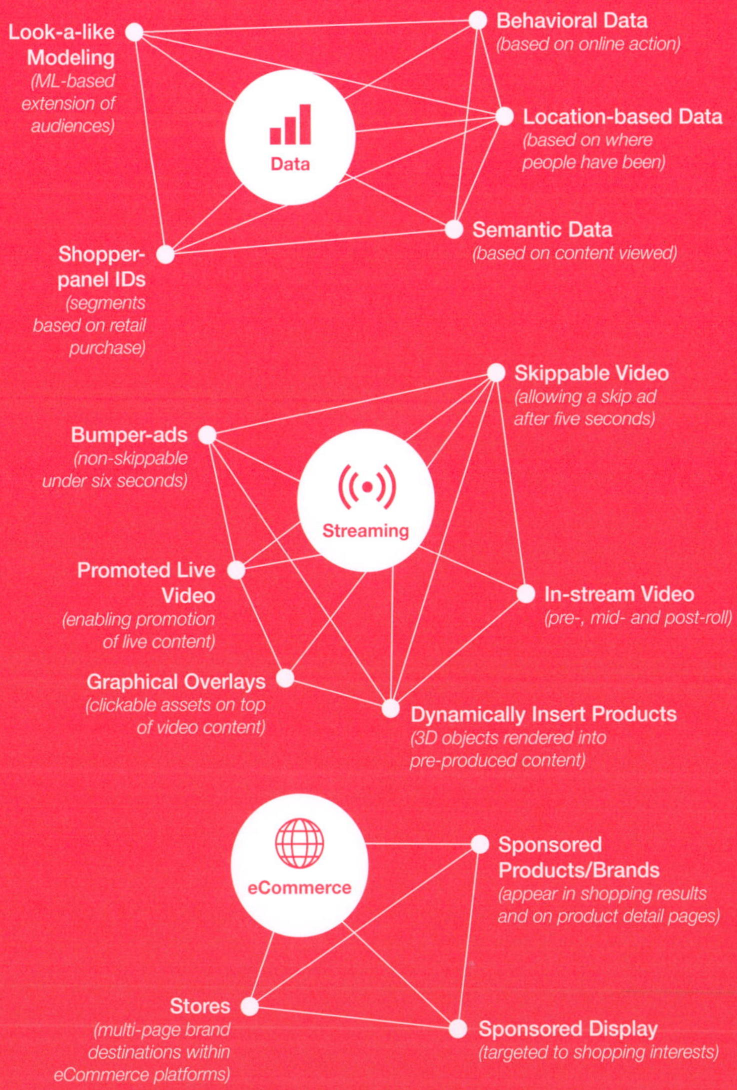
Data
Look-a-like Modeling
(ML-based extension of audiences)
Behavioral Data
(based on online action)
Location-based Data
(based on where people have been)
Semantic Data
(based on content viewed)
Shopper-panel IDs
(segments based on retail purchase)
Streaming
Skippable Video
(allowing a skip ad after five seconds)
Bumper-ads
(non-skippable under six seconds)
Promoted Live Video
(enabling promotion of live content)
In-stream Video
(pre-, mid- and post-roll)
Graphical Overlays
(clickable assets on top of video content)
Dynamically Insert Products
(3D objects rendered into pre-produced content)
eCommerce
Sponsored Products/Brands
(appear in shopping results and on product detail pages)
Stores
(multi-page brand destinations within eCommerce platforms)
Sponsored Display
(targeted to shopping interests)

The development of these five areas led to significant changes to the practice of marketing communications. This started with a digital revolution as marketers got to grips with a new range of ad placements and targeting techniques which led to an increase in digital spend and, in turn, the dramatic rise of the major digital ads platforms. The explosive growth of these digital goliaths gave them major influence over the marketing industry in general, and as they came to constitute the very infrastructure of the industry, the course of its future. All these changes created opportunities in equal measure to challenges, many of which the industryis still grappling with today.

Let's explore these events in more detail starting with the digital revolution'.

A Revolution in Ads Marketplaces: New Formats and Fresh Perils.

The huge shift in consumer attention to digital platforms did not just transfer the old ad marketplaces to new formats; it created a revolution in advertising. The tremendous shift to IP-based ad platforms enabled four key departures from the old world of advertising: total flexibility; increased ad variety; personalized ads; and abundant ads with dynamic pricing.

Total Flexibility

Total flexibility of expenditure is a key feature of these new large digital platforms, made possible because they rely on real-time auction systems to price and allocate inventory. Prior to the long decade, the only significant ad spend occurring on an auction basis was search.

At the end of 2020, the majority of digital media, inclusive of search, social, programmatic and an increasing share of connected TV advertising was being transacted via an auction mechanism.

Despite the dry nature of the subject matter, the use of auctions was not merely a technical detail: it reshaped the nature of ad markets. Without an auction system, an advertiser that cuts its budget at the last minute would create unsold inventory on the publisher side and a revenue loss—hence the restrictive cancellation terms that characterized the ad industry before the long decade. Subsequently, thanks to the use of auction systems, an advertiser that cuts its budget simply ceases to bid into a stream of ad auctions and would almost certainly be replaced by other bidding advertisers. That reduces the revenue pressure on the sell-side, enabling the tremendous flexibility that advertisers now enjoy when buying these formats.

Increased Ad Variety

Increased ad variety has also been a feature of the new ad ecosystem with the most obvious examples being the Feed ad format pioneered by Facebook and the Stories format invented by Snap. But it is just as important to look at how the departure from a broadcast schedule enabled innovation by streaming video providers. Consider YouTube, on the surface, its ad profile might appear to be the same as traditional TV—a given number and length of ad spots for an hour of programming. But nothing could be further from the truth. The flexibility of the platform allows for content of an arbitrary length, and grants content creators the freedom to insert ad breaks where they deem fit. Further still, ad breaks can expand and shrink on a per-user basis, driven by both ad demand and models of how ad load affects content consumption.

We have also seen the rapid growth of commerce-based ad formats, and increasingly all advertising has become wired for transaction. Combined with sophisticated targeting and product recommendations advertisers are better able to fulfill consumers' unmet commercial needs. These commerce-enabled ad units reduce both the consumer's level of effort, i.e. one click purchase, and time to purchase without a complex purchase experience.

In the US alone e-retail sales, as a percentage of total sales, increased 10 percentage points to 27 percent over the course of the first 10 months of the pandemic—10 years of change in 10 months. And with that came a scramble to focus more on eCommerce marketing. This placed huge pressures on organizations to find the specialist talent. The shift to eCommerce wasn't the only accelerant. It also led to dramatic changes to media consumption, one of which posed a major threat to the ability of marketers to deliver broadcast level reach.

The trend was also observed across APAC with a large number of markets experiencing significant growth on retailer platforms, driven by a range of touchpoints including social commerce and growth in older audiences who utilized eCommerce for the first time.

Personalized Ads

These new platforms enabled the massive scaling of CRM data, combined with online-behavioral data, to achieve an impact previously only dreamed of. Historically, a typical direct mail CPM ranged from $50 to $300. Today, advertisers can reach the same customer base for $8 or less on the major digital platforms. This reduction of costs for targeted advertising by one to two orders of magnitude has lowered the barriers to market entry for many direct-to-consumer businesses that would have been economically non-viable in the prior advertising landscape.

Abundant Ads

Abundant ads with dynamic pricing are another important feature of the revolution. The abundance is a function of the huge quantity of time spent on these new digital platforms—upwards of four hours per day based on our best estimates—as well as the high and generally increasing ad load placed on them. On Facebook, for example, which makes most of its money from News Feed and Stories advertising across the Facebook and Instagram apps, the typical user sees something in the order of two ads per minute. This creates an enormous supply of ad impressions. When combined with the auction system, advertisers can efficiently target a particular subset of users without paying arbitrary audience premiums.

However, this abundance was built on a platform populated by user-generated content. To the extent that these platforms reflect human behavior, this created challenges for advertisers accustomed to a standing assumption of brand safety.

The Adjacency Challenge

This new ad marketplace was a boon to advertisers: there had never been more content to advertise against. But the internet is a mirror of humanity, and a focusing lens, too. For every community centered around benign interests like home decoration, car repair or computer tweaking, there is another centered around dark topics like racial supremacy or anti-Islam bigotry and misogyny. This created a new responsibility not just on the part of the major platforms, which have a duty to police truly toxic (as opposed to unfortunate) speech, but also on the part of advertisers. In a world where much advertising is placed against user-generated content, advertisers had to rethink ad adjacencies anew. In the past, a simple review of broadcast schedules would suffice. Suddenly, a slew of retrospective analyses and prospective controls were necessary to keep ad delivery within the bounds of a given advertiser's corporate values.

These adjacency challenges were exacerbated by *recommendation systems*, the sum of the algorithms that social media platforms used to maintain user engagement. They were designed to maximize attention, generally without concern for any negative consequences they might generate, such as political radicalization. The question the social platforms faced, and still face, was how to balance their commercial interests in driving engagement, with their moral obligation to control negative activity. Not only is content curated to the individual (i.e. newsfeeds and content recommendation systems) tougher to moderate, the algorithms, which are designed to surface the most relevant content resulted in *filter-bubbles* that reinforced existing beliefs and biases.

As the digital space matured, an increasing focus was placed on assessing the quality of media delivery, and cleaning up the digital supply chain. From removing non-human-impressions to evaluating on-target audience delivery and viewability, digital media came under the microscope of intense evaluation. This work started in the early 2010s, but really gained attention in 2017, with Marc Pritchard, Chief Marketing Officer of P&G, sharing his agenda with the wider industry. This hastened the adoption of verification- and viewability-technologies and the curation of digital inventory, with inclusion and exclusion lists.

The Rise of Influencers

The development of social media resulted in the rise of the influencer. High interest categories had always focused on influencers to generate online and offline word-of-mouth. But towards the end of the long decade the role of influencer became more significant in the minds of clients and agencies. And instead of being a strand of activity they became an essential part of how marketing communications are created and cascaded.

Henrik Wenders, Senior Vice-President of Audi Brand, summarizes this change succinctly: "You no longer communicate at an audience; you communicate with and through the audience." And this was the case for all categories irrespective of the level of interest the consumer with them. Building and managing an influencer network became an important marketing capability for many advertisers.

Behind the Paywall

Towards the end of the long decade, and accelerating as we managed through the global pandemic, we witnessed a huge shift in media time from ad-supported to ad-free environments. Of the top streaming services available globally, Netflix, Amazon Prime Video and Disney+ are almost entirely ad-free. The others have optionally ad-supported models. The growing abundance of voluminous high-quality ad-free video content has reset consumer expectations around interruptions, reducing consumer tolerance for ad breaks in their entertainments, and disrupting supply and demand dynamics across the marketplace.

Some advertisers looked to mitigate the impact this would have on reach potential by becoming more inventive with how they reached consumers that went beyond the paywall.

Procter & Gamble, in partnership with National Geographic, underwrote Activate, a six-part documentary series that highlighted the work of grassroots activists in ending cash bail, eradicating plastic pollution, and more. Each episode included P&G's role in addressing the central theme.

While closer to the traditional advertising format, Sky and NBC Universal launched Ad Smart, contextual alignment for linear TV ads. By uploading keywords, advertisers can identify semantic matches to scripted content. As an example, a car crash scene within a fictional drama would be matched to a car insurance brand which would feature as the scene concludes.

The Rise of New Ad Powers: The Platform Oligopolies.

Observers hoped that the Cambrian explosion of media, driven by the open, federated nature of the internet would lead to a golden age of perfected audience targeting, measurement and real-time decisioning. Such an interoperable environment would mean that advertisers could arbitrarily combine targeting, inventory, and measurement solutions from any set of vendors they might choose to work with. In this world, each ad exposure could be matched back to an individual, and responses to each impression could be precisely quantified.

Such a model would enable us to solve some of marketing's most critical questions with increased accuracy and understanding, allowing us to drive higher levels of ad effectiveness:

- *What was the impact of my marketing investment?*
- *Who are my most valuable audiences, and why?*
- *Where should I be investing more?*
- *Where should I be investing less?*

The greatest beneficiaries of the long decade were the large platforms that were able to capitalize on the environmental conditions created by the Cambrian explosion and deliver on the redefined consumer expectations that resulted with greater value, accuracy and speed than their competitors. But this came at the cost of the dream of interoperability—as in the potential to link third-party technologies and datasets together.

This dream remains unrealized, not because of any technological limitation but rather due to the combined forces of platform market power and counterproductive actions by well-meaning regulators. The actions of a few major platforms came to dominate both our time and advertising investment and with it set the conditions under which the marketplace continues to evolve.

The primary focus of these platforms has been generating growth by monetizing their most valuable asset—customer data—combined with superior ad experience. Over time they have limited the ability for the data they collect to be leveraged in formats outside their own ecosystem of products, to further consolidate user attention and advertiser investment.

Not only did these companies lack a commercial incentive to share their data, but governments actively discouraged it through an increased focus on consumer privacy protections, providing stricter standards on the collection, use and sharing of consumer data. In these instances, governments have erected barriers to interoperability in the name of privacy, stifling competition in an already concentrated industry.

Reductions to interoperability were not just limited to data sharing for the purposes of audience targeting and measurement, but also access to these companies' owned and operated inventory. Access to inventory was restricted for a variety of commercial reasons, but the effect was always the same—to reduce advertiser choice when it comes to buying tools. See box overleaf.

Certainly companies can, and should, act in their own commercial interests within the bounds of the law. What makes this situation remarkable is that a few players have amassed so much market power that the competitive pressures, which would ordinarily prevent against such restrictive policies, are absent.

Our new reality of digital ad platform oligopolies does confer some major advantages to advertisers; the unified product stacks produced by Facebook, Google and peer firms like Alibaba and Tencent allow for remarkably sophisticated approaches. On the other hand, the price advantages that large advertisers had become accustomed to in the traditional media world have been substantially eroded by auction-based systems. While agencies reconstruct these discounts to the greatest extent possible by aggregating client spend, the leverage brought to the negotiating table by these oligopoly firms is formidable.

The fading of the interoperability dream.

- Facebook launched Facebook Exchange (FBX) in 2012 to enable advertisers to buy Facebook media programmatically using a third-party demand-side platform (DSP). Four years later, FBX was dead, dropped in favor of Website Custom Audiences (WCA), which could only be purchased using Facebook's own tools. This change helped Facebook maximize its share of revenue, by preventing DSPs capturing any of an advertiser's budget. Viewed narrowly this change could be justified based on saving advertisers' money on supply-chain fees, but it drove up advertiser costs by making it impossible to sync up these campaigns across platforms
- Google previously sold YouTube inventory via third-party DSPs up until 2015, at which time it restricted access to its own DSPs (DV360, formerly DoubleClick Bid Manager) and Google AdWords. If an advertiser's preferred DSP is anything other than DV360 and they want to use it to buy YouTube, they are out of luck
- While Amazon did make FireTV inventory available via third-party DSPs, it has since limited this to itself and The TradeDesk, removing DataXu which was acquired by an Amazon competitor, Roku

Vertical Strategies

In previous eras of media communications, companies translated their leadership position in one media vehicle to dominate in another through horizontal strategies. For example, NBC in the US and RTL in Europe, moved from radio to television, and eventually to cable, via aggressive acquisitions. They didn't move downstream to try to dominate television production, nor did they integrate upstream to restrict availability to certain companies' TV subscribers. Even today, when Comcast (an American telco) owns NBC, customers of other telcos have no trouble accessing NBC.

But the trend of the long decade has been that of the oligopoly players assembling *vertical strategies*. See box overleaf.

Increasingly this vertical arms race became the playbook for more traditional media companies, for example, AT&T's recent acquisition of digital ads platform Appnexus, which it rebranded as Xandr. However, as they continue to represent less than 35 percent of the online ads market in the US there is pressure to establish consensus and compatibility for viable alternative solutions that provide competitive scale and value.

Instead, late in the long decade the technology companies experienced threats and restrictions in the form of government intervention. This is turning out to be a bigger challenge than the normal competitive pressure felt within most markets. See box overleaf - *Governments Get Involved*.

Marketers, powered by insights emerging from meta-analyses, started to see the digital revolution in a broader context. And with this, one by one, they started to take back control of the agenda■

This vertical strategy can be simplified to the following:

1. Compile large scale customer data assets that enable advertisers to trade on behavioral currencies *(i.e. on Amazon you can target me based on the content I consume, the products I buy and my propensity to do each in the future)*

2. Assemble diversified owned and operated content surfaces with direct distribution to consumers that fulfill distinct need-states from entertainment to transactional commerce *(i.e. Facebook Watch to Instagram Shopping)*

3. Control monetization of inventory and enable ease of access via self-service buying platforms with cross-surface optimization for scalable monetization *(i.e. automated placement optimization across Facebook & Instagram Stories)*

4. Develop measurement solutions that quantify the value and interplay across their own properties *(i.e. Google or Amazon can link the timing of OTT commercials with increase in product searches and site/store traffic down to sales as a means to attribute media impact and ultimately ROI)*

Governments Get Involved.

As we ended the long decade, governments were getting more involved in the media space, and not just in the form of privacy regulations like the GDPR and CCPA. Ongoing industry consolidation was starting to draw the attention of competition authorities in both the US and EU. Merger and acquisition activity, of the dominant players, was more likely than ever to be viewed with a skeptical eye. The laissez faire approach, which allowed Google to acquire both YouTube and DoubleClick, and Facebook to purchase both Instagram and WhatsApp, was looking to have run its course. Competition authorities also made it clear they are not content merely with thwarting these firms' M&A aspirations: a series of actions in both the US and EU indicate that regulation of core business practices is imminent.

Marketers Taking Back Control: Rebalancing Long and Short-term Focus.

According to Terry Kawaja, Chief Executive of Luma Partners, prior to the Cambrian explosion, marketers "used to plan subjective media buys based on crude age and gender metrics, make guesses on ad effectiveness and then have poor measurement data to start the next cycle." He argues that with the "advent of addressability, programmatic technologies, data collection, parsing software and (some) AI," the advances in propensity-based audience modeling, data-driven attribution, and testing via randomized control trials (RCTs) created greater accuracy and sophistication in optimizing media delivery.

However, many organizations shifted too far, too fast. In their rush to modernize, they lost sight of the bigger picture.

The slide to short-termism

With an abundance of new performance data, the marketing profession became obsessed with what could be measured. The combination of direct response-based and highly measurable ad formats with instant access to quantifiable media and business performance data created a significant shift in marketing accountability and an increasing focus on short-term activation tactics and conversion-based KPIs.

The positive side of this, which remains today, is that this enabled immediate results and optimization. And real-time reporting became a reality. However, the flip side was that the quick fix of immediate revenue impact became addictive and led to excessive investment in short-term sales driving tactics, often at the expense of building brands and maximizing profit over the long term.

The crisis of clarity that has ensued in determining the optimal balance between brand and activation was analyzed extensively within the Institute of Practitioners in Advertising's (IPA) seminal 2013 study, *The Long and the Short of It*.

Its authors, Les Binet and Peter Field, argue that: "In the long run, brand effects are the main driver of growth." While activation effects produce the "biggest sales responses in the short term (six months or less)," they tend to "decay away quickly." They say: "Brand effects are harder to measure, because they are smaller in the short term, and there is usually no direct link to sales. But brand effects decay away more slowly, and so repeated exposures can cause the base level of sales to rise." A supporting case for this, included within the IPA study, demonstrated that the use of brand-based TV led to a 40 percent increase in business impact.

Further, the report asserted that if advertisers became hooked on the immediacy of direct response tactics they were at risk of spending too much money on consumers who were already in the market, and not spending enough bringing new people into the market. Around the same time, marketers were increasingly adopting and cascading marketing science throughout their organizations.

Laws of Marketing

At a time when technological advancements were starting to enable greater sophistication in areas such as consumer segmentation and targeting, the release of Byron Sharp's *How Brands Grow* in 2010 provided an evidence-based perspective to remind marketers on the importance of, what it defined as *intelligent-mass-marketing*. This argued that successful brand growth came from penetration and this is best achieved by reaching all category buyers, and not focusing exclusively on a defined cohort.

This was one of the many marketing laws asserted by the book's author. When we asked the author about the impact of *How Brands Grow*, Byron said: "It was the first book that talked about laws—a realization, for some people, that marketing could do what medicine has done. And that many CMOs have, as a result of the impact of *How Brands Grow*, shifted the focus for their organizations from 'anything goes, fashionable theories and arguing' to decision making based on an understanding of the real world."

With this came a more forensic understanding of how marketing pays back—from the importance of need states and distinctive assets through to the reassertion of the importance of reach. As for the lasting legacy of the book, and the impact of marketing science, Byron went on to say that with it came the "realization that the fundamental job as a CMO is to drive changes in cultures and systems, when previously they thought the role was to win the most awards."

Nudged by Behavioral Science

There was a resurgence in the application of behavioral sciences—the documentation and templating of the irrational behavior of human nature. According to Richard Shotton, author of *The Choice Factory*, which explores uses of behavioral science for marketing, these principles were asserted on the industry through the application at a governmental level in various countries, such as the UK, and also through the IPA under the presidency of Rory Sutherland.

The impact of behavioral science acted as a counterpoint to the increasing advancements of digital media driven by technology and data, creating a polarization in approach. This is manifested by digital evangelists believing that everything can be solved through technology and data and marketing science evangelists cautioning that these new areas were not the panacea and were stealing the agenda away from what drives brand growth.

Whichever side of the divide people took, it was hard to argue with the evidence that was starting to emerge about the impact of an over focus on measurable metrics on long-term brand health.

The more advanced marketers were able to resolve these conflicts between targeting and mass reach, and between short-term and long-term investments. They were the ones that benefited most from this long decade, using the disruption, and the shifting sands, to accelerate ahead of their competitors.

Another 10 years of change, in 10 months

And of course, as we all know, at the very end of this long decade we experienced an additional 10 years of change, this time in 10 months. The impact of the global pandemic was not that of a change agent but that of

$\frac{x}{} = 1$
$x = Y - \frac{b}{3a}$
$g(x) = \sqrt{x(x-a)(x-b)}$
$E = mc^2$
FeS
H_2O
Ω
UP

an accelerant. It increased the speed of transformation we were already witnessing. Most developed markets, that previously saw a one percentage point increase in the percentage of sales purchased online per year, saw a 10 percentage point increase in 10 months; with close to 25 percent of all retail sales now purchased online. This placed a significant burden on marketing organizations to ramp up their eCommerce capability, with a scramble to find the talent.

There was also a similar impact on subscriber levels to Subscription Video On Demand (SVOD) services. And with that, an increase in percentage of total video viewing now happening behind a paywall with the resultant implications for marketers in the form of reduced reach and, potentially, increased CPMs. This, of course, needed to be considered within the wider context of changing behavior across all channels, with dramatic changes to channels such as cinema, and in some countries for some periods of time, out of home. Increasing the importance on multichannel reach optimization. And on top of this, newer formats such as stories and vertical video had to be taken more seriously and incorporated into the asset mix; as locked-down nations increased usage of video sharing platforms such as TikTok.

For many, when they were not on social media they were playing online games. Research from Dynata and Simon-Kucher & Partners, which surveyed 13,000 consumers across 17 global markets, reported a 30 percent increase in the number of gamers during lockdown and a 39 percent increase in spend—buying games and in game purchases. Existing platforms such as Twitch and newer platforms such as Roblox grew into mini media ecosystems in their own right, with a new array of celebrity influencers. Creating a whole new environment for marketers and agencies to get to grips with.

Add to this, we also needed to adjust to changes to society; how people's values changed. Many observations across many prediction-based reports seem to agree on three lasting impacts:

1. *More local:* greater connection to one's community
2. *More watchful:* people more concerned about illness
3. *More mindful:* people more aware of mental health and well-being issues

And of course, the small matter of working remotely and requiring new collaboration software. Also, a reconfiguring of the office environment and how we all connect together physically—office work environments reimagined as coming-together environments. The impact of this on work is a separate book in itself. And is one that we will all write over the next few years.

Reflections on a Very Long Decade

The foundational elements that were in place before the change were radically reorganized by the environmental shifts of faster networks, advances in computing power and better, cheaper displays. This led to an explosion of new features within areas such as social, data, streaming, and eCommerce, such as the newsfeed, third-party data and skippable video.

These features fundamentally changed the marketer's toolkit and changed the marketing industry. Rising complexity and sophistication changed advertising into a technology business as much as a creative business. We saw huge improvements in our ability to market to audiences, with increased targeting and measurement than before. Every business was carrying out a digital transformation and increasing their digital spend, which led to huge capital flows into the major tech companies, creating a new generation of media oligopolies.

However, this increased sophistication also brought about an overemphasis on short-termism, driven by an obsession with maximizing what was measurable. This was counterbalanced by a rising chorus of dissenters asserting the universal laws of marketing science, demanding a rebalancing and a more skeptical mindset.

We are departing the long decade with a very rich set of marketing techniques. For some, these are a remarkable toolkit for generating returns from marketing investment, and have contributed to making the industry one of the most exciting to work within. Others are simply overwhelmed by the complexity. This has led, for want of a better expression, to a kind of marketing midlife crisis. In some ways, as an industry, we are unsure about where we are and where we go next. The following chapter will examine this theme, and may even make you question whether you are in a marketing midlife crisis. And if you are, which *type* of crisis you are in—that's right, there is more than one.■

**OK, ready when you are.
The therapy session begins
when you turn the page.**

Chapter 2:

A Marketing Midlife Crisis

02

In the previous chapter, invoking the concept of the Cambrian explosion was a useful framing device to unfold a sequence of connected events. For this chapter we are going to be invoking something that is perhaps a little closer to home for some of the *older* readers of this book: the midlife crisis. Or, more specifically, a *marketing* midlife crisis. Because, we believe, this is the resultant effect of the wave of complexity that has floored us, over the last 13 years.

We will attempt to draw parallels between an individual crisis and that of what we are seeing within the marketing industry after a decade of so much change.

So, please indulge us for the first few paragraphs as we set up the nature and symptoms of a midlife crisis, before we relate them to the current state of marketing—which, by the way, includes agencies as well. After which, we will seek to chart a way through. We have even brought in some outside help in the form of a marketing therapist to give us a glimpse into the impact this is having on the consumer. But more on that shortly. Let's start with where we are right now, and that starts with a question.

How do you start a new chapter?

According to the developmental psychologist and psychoanalyst Erik Erikson there are nine chapters we all go through, typified by the major conflict we face throughout that period, and the overall outcome.

By the time we reach 18-years-old, we have gone through five of those nine chapters. The dynamic of how we develop means that as we grow older the chapters in our life become few and far between, much harder to initiate, and—as the outcomes of our development become more complex—they also become imbued with greater significance and impact on our overall mental being. The result, a midlife crisis.

The symptoms of a midlife crisis are, amongst others: a yearning for simpler times and fondness for nostalgia, a bias towards short-term decision making, dramatic behavioral changes and thoughts about infidelity; all of which are underlined by the constant comparison of oneself to others.

Just as we might experience midlife questions about our own existence, it is possible that an industry can have the same existential issues threaten its development. And that has certainly been the case given the scale and pace of change that our industry has undergone over the past decade. As Henrik Wenders of Audi Brand, puts it: "The last decade has been intense in terms of transformation, fueled by digital expansion. The fundamentals of how we communicate and understand consumers has changed as a result, and that speed and complexity will only increase."

"Speed and complexity will only increase"

Henrik Wenders
Senior Vice-President of Audi Brand

Suggesting that the symptoms of the marketing midlife crisis may persist, and even increase.

Now let's try to start to understand this condition. For diagnosis, we can see the symptoms that hold true in a personal midlife crisis, are just as evident in marketing's midlife crisis.

- Impulsive decision making

  The slide into a preference for quick-fix short-term marketing over the last decade has been to the long-term detriment of many brands. This is expressed by adam&eveDDB's Head of Effectiveness Les Binet: "All businesses can now assess short-term metrics, which can distract them from long-term growth."

- Dramatic changes in behavior and appearance

  Rebranding, as a topic of search interest over the past decade has skyrocketed—it was five times more popular as a topic of interest in November 2019 than it was ten years prior, and the growth between those two points has been consistent. But you can also see it in the language we all use.

- Thoughts about infidelity

  The latter half of the last decade has seen monumental change in the value of advertising reviews, with around $2.56 billion of global media and creative revenue changing hands in 2020 alone.

The Eight Marketing Midlife Crisis Words.

These eight words are relied on like crutches to express poorly formed thoughts. We are not judging; we are guilty ourselves.

PHD is making a commitment, as an agency, to purge these *marketing midlife crisis* words from our lexicon—with a commitment for *zero emissions by 2030*. We are going to kill one word before its even taken hold—see number seven.

Marketing Midlife Crisis Words.

With suggested replacements in italics

1	**Disruptive**	*New*
2	**Hack**	*Improve*
3	**Hyper-local**	*Local*
4	**Ideate**	*Conceive*
5	**Millennials**	*25-40 Year Olds*
6	**New-normal**	*Today*
7	**Phygital**	*Technology*
8	**Pivot**	*Change*

- An intense feeling of nostalgia and a yearning for simpler times

  Many in the industry hark back to an earlier time. With certain generations wrestling with the conflicting emotional feelings they have with the way technology and data have entered the industry.

- The constant comparison of oneself to others

  Act like a start-up is all too common a mantra for large businesses, and the allure of being more agile or nimble is too great for some. Agencies are not invulnerable from the appeal either. Suresh Balaji, Chief Marketing Officer of HSBX APAC, observes that agencies often disrupt their business model to their disadvantage: "They start to forget their core reason for existence, and they try to become a 'big four consultancy'".

The impact on relationships.

All of these symptoms also have an impact on one's relationships. Where, for people that are in relationships, they haven't kept pace with how their partner has changed and are therefore not truly seeing them. And what they need. And with this, assumptions are made about what the other person needs which can be out of sync with reality, leading to issues. This relationship breakdown is manifest in the way that marketers and the agencies consider the consumer.

To explore this further we asked Mark Ritson, marketing consultant and founder of The Mini MBA in Marketing to consider the breakdown in the relationship between marketing and the consumer through the lens of a marketing therapist. Come and be a fly on the wall in a couple's therapy session.

A MARKETING THERAPY SESSION.

By ***Mark Ritson***

There is a knock at the door. The COUNSELOR rises and opens the door. A couple smile politely and enter the room. Both sit on the sofa facing the counsellor. They seem nervous.

MARKETER, a tall, nondescript man in his early 40s, speaks first.

> *MARKETER:* It's very good of you to see us at such short notice. Where would you like us to begin?

> *COUNSELOR:* Well, why don't we start with what brought you into my office today. I'd like to hear from both of you the reasons behind this session.

CONSUMER, a well-dressed woman in her 40s, clears her throat and speaks.

> *CONSUMER:* For me it is very simple. He just does not listen to me anymore. I think back to when we first met and he was so attentive. He was obsessed with understanding everything about me. Where I came from. What I did for a living. My interests. My attitudes. My needs and how he could satisfy them. But as time passed he stopped listening to me. He thinks he knows it all. All he does is talk, talk, talk. Promoting himself. Going on about how good he is at this or at that. And he just does not spend a second thinking about me or listening to what I want. All he does is talk, he never listens.

CONSUMER stops and looks down to her hands. She is visibly angry.

MARKETER: That's easy for you to say. When we met you only had eyes for me. We talked all the time about how much you loved me. How loyal you were to me. But that has changed so much in the last 10 years. These days I do not even know if love exists between us. Is there even such a thing as loyalty anymore? You spend as much time with other people as you do with me and I just don't know if that bond, that exclusivity, still exists?

CONSUMER: If you read a bit more you'd come to understand that I am just doing what everyone else is doing. As Byron Sharp puts it…

MARKETER: Who the fuck is Byron?! The guy from the gym? Is he that guy? Is he? Is he? What does he have that I cannot offer you? You see what I deal with? No wonder I feel so insecure.

COUNSELOR: OK, let's track back a little. Marketer, you say you are insecure. Tell me about that.

MARKETER: I will admit that I have a lot of concerns about performance these days. A lot of the time it is all I think about. And I worry—again all the time—that my performance is letting me down.

CONSUMER: That's because you are obsessed with the internet. I keep telling him not to watch those videos. All that unrealistic, fake stuff. It's not real!

But he is glued to it and it gives him silly ideas. His performance is fine. But I need to feel loved first. To feel special. To feel like you are there for me. If that long-term stuff is in place, then the short-term stuff will work out beautifully. Make me feel the emotion first, and I bet your performance will be more than good enough. But all you think about is short-term gratification and it does not do it for me.

MARKETER: You are not being fair. I use all those new toys to spice things up in our relationship. You want new stuff, and I get all that stuff off the internet and give it to you. You love all the exotic, innovative stuff I have brought into the relationship. You cannot get enough.

CONSUMER: I admit I like to keep things fresh but a lot of the stuff is underwhelming. Some of it is just plain silly. I'm a traditional girl at heart and you just don't seem interested in the more physical aspects of our relationship anymore. It's always "come and look at this on the internet" or "look at how they do it on TikTok." I miss the intimacy of just being with you in a physical space. Just me and you. The digital stuff is nice. But I like it traditional too. I love a simple, basic position for example.

MARKETER: But I have so many positions I want to try out. I can do it so many different ways.

CONSUMER: I don't want six different positions. Just the one traditional position. You know the one. It delivers every time and speaks to my physical and emotional needs. But you are always flapping about trying to add more fancy new positions that you learned from your mates or read about online. You are losing me with all that stuff. You are all over the place. You don't know who you are anymore.

MARKETER: But it's about personalization. About going further to deliver exactly what you want. Can't you see that?

CONSUMER: Honestly, that's just BS off the internet. You don't need to know everything. I keep catching you looking at my phone and checking out the websites I have been visiting. It creeps me out. I feel like you are obsessed with things that are of no relevance. I just like it the way I've always liked it. The way most people like it.

MARKETER: You have changed. When we were younger you used to focus on me, just me. But your attention is all over the place these days. You hardly sit down and watch TV with me like you used to. And when you do it's always the subscription channels and you know I can't get into those. And when you are not on Netlfix it's your smartphone and there is no way I can break through there. How am I supposed to connect with you any more?

CONSUMER: I admit I am more diverse in my habits these days compared to 20 years ago. But you exaggerate. I still watch TV most nights but I'm usually on my own these days. You are too busy on Instagram or Twitter to notice. Or you're next door talking to Trey the fitness instructor because you think he is a 'positive influence' on me. No-one listens to him except you. Can't you see that? He is a joke.

MARKETER: Trey is a big part of my life these days. Since he moved in next door I've come to depend on him. And I'm not the only one. He has told me about all the ways he has helped you to come round to my way of thinking. If it wasn't for Trey I do not know what I would do.

CONSUMER: Trey is a dickhead. And he makes you look like a dickhead too. Face the facts, you are having a massive midlife crisis. You just sit there for hours going on about the need to find your 'purpose'. WTF?! I am right here. Stop being so over-dramatic and indulgent. Get a grip!

MARKETER: I admit it. I am a little lost. I think about little else other than purpose. Everybody tells me I need to find one. But I can see how that has gotten in the way of me thinking more about you and what you need.

CONSUMER: There is still hope for us. I'm still very attracted to you. And I'm still the same person I always was. You just need you to focus on the basics and ignore all the nonsense from your mates. Keep it simple. Listen to me. Understand my needs. Stop looking for new gimmicks and focus on what has always worked in the past. I am still here for you.

MARKETER: Do you really mean that? Because I want you more than ever. Especially since Covid hit.

CONSUMER: I really do. As David Ogilvy once said…

MARKETER: Who the fuck is David?

Mark Ritson is a columnist, marketing consultant and founder of The Mini MBA in Marketing.

The impact on marketing.

All of these symptoms are having an impact on the day-to day functional health of the patient. Fundamental to the detriment of that health, is the conflict of opinion amongst marketers and agencies about the most effective way of generating marketing payback. In so many areas of our life over the past decade we have witnessed a polarization and entrenchment of debate. Arguments have become binary and reductive, based on tribal lines, and debate has become reduced into single-word issues: pro or anti, yes or no, leave or remain, for example. The world of marketing has not been immune from the polarization of debate either. The last long decade of marketing has seen many of the symptoms of the midlife crisis exacerbated by polarization but never really addressed, often caused by different stakeholders in different positions with different priorities.

As Rory Sutherland, Vice-Chairman of Ogilvy UK, famously said: "Talking to a Finance Director about brand iconography is like going to the head surgeon at St. Mary's Hospital and suggesting they trust in the healing power of crystals."

A casual look at the industry through social media reveals disagreement over even seemingly straightforward definitions. Much of this debate falls to the comparison between brand and activation: whether it is more fundamental to establish a brand over the long term, or whether the focus should be on acquiring efficiently in the short term. And there are marketing organizations that naturally—due to their life stage—fall on either side of the divide.

In the 2017 publication *Marketing Effectiveness in the Digital Era*, Les Binet and Peter Field highlight their findings that "effectiveness has declined since the global financial crisis… marketers need to strike a better balance between short and long term if they want to exploit the full potential of marketing in today's media landscape." Even for organizations that feel they have resolved the conflict and talk in terms of full-funnel marketing, the pressure on the short-term needs of the business can lead to over-investments in the lower funnel, and/or top-funnel brand advertising being judged based on lower-funnel metrics. Top funnel brand advertising is also commonly the first to be cut when budget pressures arise.

Take the Automobile Association (the AA) in the UK, for example, in its award-winning case study *From Spark Plugs, to Singalongs*. As a business it had become increasingly focused on efficient delivery of short-term results, and business by their measures was doing well. The AA's profit was growing steadily, average renewal value had increased by 40 percent and its marketing costs had decreased by more than 50 percent from their peak. However, a look underneath the bonnet of these top-line figures reveals a different story, one of decreasing brand salience, search volume and declining membership.

A dramatic overhaul to its marketing strategy then took place; a rebalance towards brand-driven marketing. In the short term the AA had to hold its nerve, but it was worth it. Within three years, the AA completely transformed its revenue model: from artificially low acquisition prices and inflated renewal fees, to creating sustainable revenue growth through higher demand at higher prices. With this turnaround strategy, ROI was increased by thirty percent, and market share increased during the period by three percentage points.

This case study of marketing redemption is a pertinent reminder to marketers across the world on the perils of focusing on the wrong data points, or at least certain data points in the absence of others because they are easier to measure. Andrew Robertson, Worldwide Chief Executive Officer of BBDO, points out: "It was Sir John Banham, former head of the Confederation of British Industry, who said: 'we are in danger of placing the greatest importance to the things we can measure most easily, and thus ensuring we are precisely wrong rather than roughly right'."

"The concern is that the vast dollars of global marketing spend are being spent by non-marketers who view marketing as a parody of classical economics: that brands don't matter; consumer choice is rational; we work with perfect information; consumers maximize utility; and everything is rationally evaluated."

Les Binet
Head of Effectiveness at adam&eveDDB

Linked to the battle between prioritizing the short or long-term, is an overly mechanistic view of how marketing works. As Les Binet mentions:

The creative work that results from this approach will only exacerbate the prevalence of ad avoidance and the reported decline of both awareness and creative effectiveness. Arguably, the over-focus on this machine-like, short-term approach to marketing is the biggest destroyer of corporate value that marketing, and advertising, has ever had. However, close behind that will be over-investments in marketing technologies that offer low levels of utility for the type of business.

For example, companies that are in low-consideration categories, where people do not do *any* online research prior to purchase, invested significant amounts of money into CRM-based marketing platforms. They commit huge amounts of money to have access to a Data Management Platform from which third-party audience segments are created but which represent only a tiny fraction of the category buyer base.

This situation has been exacerbated by the persuasive power of marketing conferences where a disproportionate level of importance has been placed upon marketing and advertising technology. This is further reinforced by the FOMO effect (fear of missing out) caused by new entrants (both brands *and* agencies) emerging without any of the legacy mindsets and infrastructure of the incumbents. These are often much quicker to leverage marketing technology and digital media technology that has levelled the playing field for start-up businesses. Daryl Simm, the Global Chief Executive of Omnicom Media Group, says: "The financial barriers to entry have been lowered for the more agile, or flexible. Suddenly you don't need significant capital to create something."

Many start-up, or scale-up, businesses are led by marketers who wouldn't necessarily identify themselves as marketers. They deal directly with technology vendors and media vendors, and likely see themselves as customers of platforms (many of which are self-serve), and not as the clients of agencies. Due to the early life stage of their business, they *tend* to be focused on efficiently acquiring customers (activation) and prioritizing cashflow versus more long-term brand building activities.

The large gains these smaller businesses are seeing—again, because they are in a rapid growth phase of their business—cause ripples and disruption not only to business models, but they also seem to vindicate the successful use of short-term marketing. The symptom of comparing oneself to others is as prevalent as it is destructive, as Daryl Simm indicates: "Marketers are being held back by the constant comparison of their business to the smaller, more agile businesses."

With the conflict, complexity, and concern of missing out, there is no wonder that the industry spiraled into the midlife crisis.

We are going to suggest that to successfully navigate a way out we need to begin by identifying which *type* of midlife crisis one's organization is in; and we have attempted to categorize them. The following five midlife crisis archetypes apply to agency and marketing organizations alike.

Let's start with The King Henry VIII.

1. The King Henry VIII ('Let's change everything')

What is it?

Imagine ruling a country for 38 years, establishing the Royal Navy and performing radical changes to the English constitution, and the thing people best remember you for is all the marriages you had?

King Henry VIII was restless and relentless. Forcing through change at any cost. Causing a lot of collateral damage.

The marketing equivalent is a pitch-shaped corporate battering ram that cleaves through agency holding groups ceaselessly for the one thing they are desperately searching for.

What are the warning signs?

The marketing equivalent may unleash slightly less grief with its constant changing of agencies, renegotiation of terms, or changes to long-term strategy, but the frenetic search that takes place is still destructive.

According to marketing consultancy R3, the number of global reviews in 2020 increased by 24 percent compared to 2015; a symptom that constant searching is increasingly becoming an industry reality.

How does one manage with it?

The underlying motivation behind King Henry VIII's hunt for an heir was to shore up a dynasty. Spending time to truly understand the ambiguous or misunderstood intentions that lie behind The King Henry VIII organization's frenzied pursuit is the only way to avoid a corporate annulment (or worse, a beheading).

For marketing organizations, it is really important that they are clear with their own marketing strategy before engaging external partners. Any internal lack of clarity, vision, and stakeholder alignment is rarely resolved just through engagement with external partners.

Equally, the intent behind any agency change needs further consideration and rigor applied to it, as David Indo, Global Chief Executive and co-founder of management consultancy ID Comms has found: "Many businesses are still dealing with legacy issues, they view media as a commodity, they are overburdened by procurement, and in the throes of an addiction to reduce cost rather than maximize value." Only if agency leadership lacks the required commitment, clarity and vision should a pitch be considered.

Once clear, organizations, working with their agency partners, should focus on the definition and acquisition of the talent required and focus on making themselves a priority client for their agency, David Indo advises: "You can't change your billings or geographical remit, but that's only one axis. If you are a client who is invested in media, is inclusive and focuses on delivering the very best strategic briefs, then you're going to rise to the top. Brands can't change who they are, but they can change their behavior."

2. The Madonna ('What's the new thing?')

What is it?

Throughout her phenomenal 40-year career Madonna has been a byword for constant reinvention. It is the only way for longevity and success in the transient world of pop music, to consistently stay on top of trends, presenting your offering as relevant and of-the-moment.

The organization equivalent aspires towards consistent relevance, not only for their viewpoints but in their output. Unfortunately, and unlike Madonna, this organization's reinvention often misses the mark. It is giddying to observe the breakneck-speed of trend-spotting decisions being made as the organization attempts to navigate a shifting landscape.

What are the warning signs?

The Madonna marketing organization aims to reinvent the fundamentals of its marketing approach to suit every, and absolutely any, pathway. The downside is that it is done at an absolute whim, with a bewildering regularity, and each change of direction utterly misses the bullseye. From TV to mobile to blockchain to crypto and back to TV again, all in the blink of an eye.

Agencies are particularly guilty of falling into this trap, becoming carried away with creating their *must-see* trends presentation for the year, only to find them padded out with tenuous predictions, some of which are at odds with real day-to-day observable consumer behavior.

How does one manage with it?

The difficulty with The Madonna organization is that invariably amongst the mad flurry of trend-gazing documents, at least some of it might become accurate. After all, change is inevitable, but not at the rate this archetype thinks.

As scattergun as many of the proposed reinventions of our industry seem, it is important to identify and prepare for major changes. As Audi's Henrik Wenders states: "You don't need to hop on every new hipster thing, but you do have to be open-minded to change." Keeping the considered balance between opportunity and reality is a key attribute to making the absolute best of every new marketing innovation or trend. Andrew Robertson observes that: "Agencies and clients need to learn to be more obsessed with people, rather than consumers in a category. We're all guilty of looking at category data then layering a bit of personal stuff on top. That's not how people live."

Obsessions about nascent or niche concepts that don't necessarily have a significant potential for revenue impact, are most often caused by substituting a lack of clarity on KPIs for the excitement of jumping on the bandwagon, as Debasree Dasgupta, Marketing Director for Pepsi West Europe, notes: "Everybody wants to be a part of the conversation, but you need to understand: how does it really impact from a consumer perspective; how is it really consistent for the brand; and how is it really connected to the product?"

All too often, technology can be seen as the end rather than just the means, Debasree Dasgupta continues: "Technology has been great ammunition for the marketer, but you still need a blueprint and understanding of how to use it effectively."

If your organization presents this symptom it is most likely an indication that there is a need to improve the linking of marketing input to marketing output: linking media KPI to marketing KPI to business KPI in a causally linked analytical model. This will floodlight the entire marketing machine and enable people to stay focused on activities that actually contribute towards growth.

3. The Christopher Columbus ('Where are we going?')

What is it?

Some of history's most exalted explorers have meticulously and successfully planned their journeys to new destinations, and others…not so much. Christopher Columbus, for example, famously set off to find a route to the Far East, but instead ended up in The Bahamas.

Within marketing organizations this can manifest itself similarly; those that seem to be operating without a map or sense of direction, unsure of where they will eventually end up. Many map-making activities seem to be getting lower and lower on the priority list, according to a 2020 survey of CMOs by Gartner which revealed that activities like market research are only a top three priority for one in four CMOs, and with customer research even less so, with only 14 percent agreeing it would fall into their top three priorities.

What are the warning signs?

It is forgivable that some of the original explorers—who were *literally* in uncharted waters—ended up in destinations that they didn't originally intend. But it is less excusable for an agency or marketing organization to have to rely on sheer luck to get where they are going.

It is unlikely that pinning hope on serendipity achieving effectiveness is a good or successful marketing strategy.

How does one manage with it?

We have a great advantage over historical explorers. Industry research has already explored the waters and where it has not—in activities such as zero-based budgeting—we have the equivalent of satellite photography, such as historical market mix modeling, to help chart a way through. Using the tools at our disposal will always help chart what we don't understand and create a more accurate plan for how to get to our destination.

As well as the obvious fix of setting very clear goals, there is also an additional requirement to help manage through with this archetype; as with the early explorers, having an accurate map is an essential component for effective navigation.

The marketing equivalent is making sure the organization has an accurate understanding of the laws of marketing science, how marketing investment actually leads to brand growth, and work to these in brand and campaign development. This will ensure there is less variability in the impact of marketing investment. Which nicely segues into the next archetype.

4. The Donald ('Listen to me')

What is it?

A name that has become synonymous with one man, Donald Trump. A man, who is the living embodiment of the Dunning-Kruger effect (a hypothetical cognitive bias where people with low self-awareness believe they are smarter and more capable than they really are). Who, amongst other utterly incredulous decisions, once advocated for "bringing light inside the body" or for injecting bleach into a patient's bloodstream as a treatment for COVID-19.

Similarly, The Donald organization can profess an understanding of marketing science and might even quote some of the most salient insights liberally. Sadly, they are unlikely to have taken the understanding much further than the surface-level to deeply inform their marketing strategy.

We asked Les Binet why, even though anecdotally we are surrounded by people using such studies along with other industry research, do we not see more people following their findings. He responded: "Simply put, there are many marketers and many organizations that are simply not aware of it. In terms of social influence, Binet and Field pale in comparison to the size of following that a Mark Ritson or a Byron Sharp has, and they pale in comparison to a Gary Vaynerchuck. The sources of information that people have readily available guides their decision making."

With so much research into marketing effectiveness from academia, case studies from industry bodies or award entries, the information to improve strategies abounds. But too often a superficial understanding prevails. And in some cases, there may be a resistance to these new marketing insights as they contradict earlier assertions by the organization.

What are the warning signs?

Professing a deep and profound knowledge from only reading the gist of something is, of course, nothing new. According to a 2016 study, only 59 percent of the links shared on social media are actually read before they are reshared. That unguided sharing of knowledge has put pressure on social media platforms to institute new measures to confirm someone has read an article before sharing its contents. This is likely to be the same for marketing studies. In both arenas, marketing and social media, it is an understandable attempt to feign knowledge and keep an air of authority at speed. But it is best avoided. There is, of course, another warning sign and that is lower than expected organic growth compared to competitors with parity products that are practicing the laws of marketing science.

How does one manage with it?

The best way to manage through this archetype is to make marketing science insights more relevant to the commercial realities of the business. Relating the industry fundamentals back to the specific business problem and circumstances The Donald organization finds itself in, will work to its good intentions, making the insights more relevant and therefore more absorbable.

If there is a deeper resistance due to the aforementioned conflict with previously asserted views about how marketing works, then the task is greater.

5. The Harry Houdini ('It's magic')

What is it?

The famous escape artist and illusionist Harry Houdini created awe and intrigue around every appearance. There is a parallel in marketing (and agencies) too. Many of us will be familiar with organizations entrenched in using bewildering jargon and buzzwords, or creating solutions intended to solve problems that were previously thought inescapable or intractable. Presented as magic, this marketing *solution* seemingly disappears almost as quickly as it arrives, leaving everyone confused and wondering what happens next. One of the motivational drivers of The Harry Houdini is to confound their audience. Hence this archetypal organization tends to be drawn to complexity.

What are the warning signs?

Organizations and agencies that have moved very quickly into the technology space and invested in a technology-vendor relationship that is far more sophisticated than the organization needs are frequently guilty of this. Internal stakeholders are often compelled to celebrate the advancements, repeating back the magical sounding buzzword, in order to prove they are ahead of a curve that might not even exist.

In order to diagnose this archetype, one has to look very carefully at the organization because there are many instances where the technology will be having a significantly positive effect on the business. One thing to look for is whether or not there is a conscious or unconscious desire to not have to think too hard about the hard stuff. True strategic thinking is difficult. According to Dave Trott, Creative Director, copywriter and author, this in part, explains the obsession with technology. "What everyone is doing is looking for a way to stop thinking…we've become fixated on the form of advertising, not the function."

How does one manage with it?

If it appears that an organization is suffering from the characteristics of this archetype—building solutions that are presented as magic but are actually overly complex activities and investments that don't pay back—the magician's curtain needs to be pulled back and the secrets revealed.

"In marketing, you are now in the translation business. You have to constantly translate expert knowledge into a language that the customer and the decision makers understand."

Stefan Buescher,
Chief Marketing Officer of the Volkswagen Group

Applying a simplifying mindset in order to see the investments more clearly is essential here and putting in place expertise that can be effective translators of complexity. Stefan Buescher, Chief Marketing Officer of the Volkswagen Group, says that translation is the key attribute in solving the problem of marketing comprehension. "In marketing, you are now in the translation business. You have to constantly translate expert knowledge into a language that the customer and the decision makers understand". Without that ability to translate our marketing understanding, we act as if we are hiding behind the magician's curtain: using indecipherable jargon to mask a lack of clarity.

These five archetypes capture most of the characteristics observable within the marketing industry as it works its way through its midlife crisis. There may well be others, or refinements, of the five. But what is important is that we start to think clearly and honestly about the dysfunctional behaviors of marketing and their downstream effects in maintaining legacy structures and inhibiting effectiveness. As BBDO's Andrew Robertson puts it: "One of the things that surprises me the most is how companies that really do know better still do, what I regard, as the wrong thing. This highlights the power of culture. It would never happen in a business that was starting from scratch".

Sometimes you have to destroy something in order to build something better. The midlife crisis for marketing is an opportunity to shatter any anxieties that are holding the organization back because as Stefan Buescher points out: "Anxiety has never been an engine for positive change". ■

The Five Marketing Midlife Crises Archetypes.

	The King Henry VIII	**The Madonna**
	CHANGE EVERYTHING	WHAT'S NEW?
PRIMARY CONDITION:	Dissatisfaction	Distraction
HOW TO SPOT IT:	Continual and abrupt changes to the agenda *(with implication for personnel and agencies)*	An overfocus on the next big thing *(at the expense of what drives the business, today)*
PRACTICAL SOLUTIONS:	Assessment of Best-in-class *(and skill gaps — to create a realistic point of comparison and perspective for change)*	Build measurement framework *(linking all marketing input to marketing output)*
DESIRED OUTCOME:	Everyone *informed* making fewer but better decisions	Everyone *focused* on activities that actually contribute

NB: Applies to Organizations that Carry-out Marketing and Agencies'

The Christopher Columbus	**The Donald**	**The Harry Houdini**
WHERE ARE WE GOING?	LISTEN TO ME	LOOK AT THIS!
Disarray	Delusion	Denial
Little/no understanding on where the business is heading *(and the role for marketing)*	Unsupported and unevidenced dogma on how marketing works	Confounding with complexity and 'magic-solutions' *(that do not have claimed impact)*
Create long-term vision *(with road-map and how marketing contributes to this)*	Investment in learning *(into marketing science—starting with leaders first)*	Institutionalize feedback *(so leaders can understand real world impact and/or employees are skilled)*
Everyone *clear* on the way forward	Everyone *enlightened* on how marketing works	Everyone *heard* and on the same page

So how do you get out of a marketing midlife crisis?

It starts with each of us, with our own introspection. So far, this chapter has been about the organizational midlife crisis. Before we discuss how to help the organization it is worth a moment to think about the individual. About the role that we all play. All of the symptoms of a marketing midlife crisis are created by many different things but perhaps there is one underlying cause—a misalignment of focus. To what extent is the focus on protecting and propelling one's own career versus protecting and propelling the business. If the focus is on the former, individuals within that organization will create one of the archetypes as set out earlier in this chapter.

For these organizations it is really important to floodlight this as an issue. To make people aware that this is a condition of the organization. And understand its roots. Mostly coming from a place of anxiety. And anxiety
is often caused by ambiguity.

The aim is for people to be clear about their position within, and their contribution to, the organization. Clear KPIs linked to each individual is an important element to build into the business. So that people are promoted based on contribution not based on how good people *think* they are.

Having achieved enlightenment at an individual level, it is now possible to turn attention to the organization within which one works, be that at a marketing organization or agency.

Ask yourself "what is your organization's reason for existing, beyond money?" Being able to answer that question clearly is an important first step (and *Shift* will explore this in further depth as we move into Chapter 4). But for now, it is an important question to ask as it will act as the guiding path out of a midlife crisis. Achieving clarity and alignment about one's own organizational mission must be prioritized over obsessing about others. As Suresh Balaji from HSBC says: "Focusing on someone else's business means you're not focusing on your own."

"Focusing on someone else's business means you're not focusing on your own."

Suresh Balaji
Chief Marketing Officer of HSBC APAC

Marketing leadership, according to Audi's Henrik Wenders, is about progress. "A reliance to keep the business 'steady' or to protect the *status quo* seems to be holding back a lot of marketing efforts—it's not about managing the *status quo*." Decision making should therefore lead to progress.

Clarity on the mission is only the first step. The next step is to plan for the longer term. According to *The Wall Street Journal* the average CMO tenure is now three years and four months. Within that window the average Autos, Confectionery, Consumer Electricals or Leisure and Entertainment business in the UK would have increased their consideration by only 0.35 percent. Growing brand strength takes time and without a consistent long-term strategy you can risk losing significant momentum.

The next step is to put in place the measurement framework. It helps to work with as clear a picture as possible through a linked measurement system that combines short- and long-term impacts. This will enable more effective day-to-day decision making.

Only at this point does it make sense to bring in external support as the vision, long-term plan and measurement infrastructure is clear. Therefore, the requirement for external contribution can be clearly defined, *and assessed*.

It is critical at this stage to manage the *how* of the working relationship with partners, and to engineer a positive environment for change, one that creates a psychologically-safe environment for the extended team. As Patricia Corsi, Global Chief Marketing and Digital Officer at Bayer, puts it: "Creating a safe environment for conflict through honesty and transparency is critical. Consensus is the death of creativity, there is a belief amongst some that collaboration equals consensus. But that's not true."

External partners must also help develop the functioning of the marketing organization. In a fast-moving landscape of complexity, companies need to evolve to survive. Stefan Buescher advocates that marketers need to be "surrounded with a network of experts that they can trust to keep them updated."

This is particularly important as the marketing world becomes increasingly more complex. With an increasingly heterogeneous set of marketing services, covered by an increasing number of specialist agencies, there is a risk of fragmentation of control, leading to disintegrated campaigns.

According to Conny Braams, Chief Digital and Marketing Officer at Unilever: "Teams that manage agencies and marketing processes in silos, run the risk of ultimately fragmenting the consumer experience. When you work as an integrated team internally and with your agency partners, consistently, it creates the right foundation for brilliance in purposeful branding, outstanding creativity, breakthrough innovation and superior growth."

However, the question of how marketers bring external partners in has become more complex as the scope of services offered by agencies has extended.

Some functions are better housed within marketing organizations whereas some are better outsourced to agencies. Some functions are best hubbed where the expertise can be found, and some may be better offshored where efficiencies can be gained.

What is clear is that, as we emerge from the midlife crisis, we really need to think about how to better organize ourselves.

That is what we are going to focus on next: how to create a healthier functioning ecosystem. It is time to turn over a new leaf, literally and metaphorically.▪

Chapter 3:

03

Building A New Ecosystem

By now you may be feeling the weight of the marketing midlife crisis. The good news is that there is a way through this. And we are going to do it together, starting now, with Chapter 3.

We are going to consider how we can reorganize ourselves more effectively: to create a healthier functioning system. And we aim to do this in two steps.

First, is to make sure that strong and healthy foundations are in place. To help organize our thinking we have defined five areas that need to be considered to make sure the fundamentals are in place. We will look at each of the five in turn, in order to get clarity on what is needed for a basic level of health—irrespective of the type of organization.

Second, once organizations have strong foundations, they can start to think about how to develop further, for the future. This future development will, of course, be unique to each organization. In order to make sense of the almost unlimited variation of organization, we have created a matrix.

This matrix will, we hope, help individuals identify the type of organization that they work within, and how it could evolve based on the characteristics of how the business functions.

Finally, we will tackle the big debate in marketing structures head on—in-housing vs. outsourcing. Including a view from someone who has been on both sides of the fence.

One more thing to say before we start; our commitment to you is we will endeavor not to slip into marketing jargon. Partly because it can be quite annoying, but mostly because it makes the subject matter much harder to digest.

Okay, let's start by looking at the foundations. All five of them.

The Five Foundations.

The result of our discussions with clients is a growing conviction that marketing departments and agencies need to rethink the way they are structured, including how the different elements of a marketing organization work together with the agency. The five foundations that need to be considered are as follows:

1 **Technology**

2 **Capability**

3 **Process**

4 **Insight**

5 **Measurement**

NB: Insight and Measurement could be seen as a subset of the first three. However, we have pulled them out as separate foundations as they have a significant impact on the business and therefore justify the individual focus.

The way each one is treated can, and should, be very different across each unique organization—a large tech conglomerate might need a more complex tech ecosystem than a dairy brand, for example—and we will talk about that a bit later. For now, we want to explore each of these five at a generic level. Starting with how they look when they are not optimized. You might recognize some of the symptoms:

Unhealthy Organizations and Agencies:

Foundation	Assessment	Indicators
1. Technology	Inflexible	Outdated legacy technology that creates inefficiencies (and that is not 'interoperable'). 'Vendor-lock'—contracts with external technology providers that hold the company back.
2. Capability	Constrained	Employees deskilling as the practice of marketing communications becomes more advanced. A lack of funding for external marketing expertise.
3. Process	Cumbersome	Outdated processes kept in place to protect jobs. Processes to solve for a poorly structured organization.

Foundation	Assessment	Indicators
4. Insight	Narrow	Data is limited to PowerPoint charts. Data that is not impacting optimization and measurement.
5. Measurement	Limiting	Focusing on KPIs that are not linked to growth (for example, ROI). Different departments focusing on competing KPIs (brand vs. short-term).

It is most likely that all of us have had experience of the optimized state of each of the five. And many of us will still be experiencing this today. The question is how we move forward. What does the optimized state look like? Let's take a look.

Healthy Organizations and Agencies:

Foundation	Assessment	Indicators
1. Technology	Empowering	Marketing and advertising technology platforms that free people up, giving them more time back for thinking. Inspire people with information and guidance to help them perform at a higher level.
2. Capability	Regenerative	Highly curious organizations that focus a lot on upscaling their workforce in the evolving areas of marketing communications. Bringing in new expertise to keep advancing the capability.
3. Process	Agile	Processes that empower people to make decisions (reduced lines of command). Technology platforms improve speed and foster collaboration.

An important objective, beyond the direct impact of revenue-growth, is for technology to liberate people, freeing them up from day-to-day tasks.

---

2 Capability: *That Can Evolve*

The next chapter will explore how we go about empowering a company's most important asset—its people—given that we have arguably been guilty of placing too much emphasis on technology and data, and not enough on them. How people and technology come together is critical, but this interplay is always changing. It is, therefore, difficult to pinpoint exactly what skills organizations will need to embed over the next three to five years, but we can say with some certainty that these will be different from those commonly found today.

Gerhard Louw, Global Head of Media at Lindt & Sprüngli, undertook a reorganization of the paid media set-up at Deutsche Telekom. He reflected that "one of our biggest gaps was having people with the right level of expertise to evaluate how to best use the data we have, so we used some internal people but also consultants and other experts to help us build a longer-term vision. These people also helped us to bring the defined set-up to life."

Managing an increasingly diverse range of different specialist agencies, albeit all part of one holding company, is a necessary reality as marketing becomes more specialized. As Polly Cochrane, WarnerMedia UK & Ireland country manager, comments: "It is almost impossible for just one agency to be able to answer all questions." And further reinforcing the need for external support in the specialist areas: "There is an agency for every facet of marketing now, it's so complicated. There's much more of an onus on the client-side marketing teams to orchestrate the whole than there was in the days of full-service agencies."

In order to create a capability that can evolve it is important that leadership functions within the organization are in place for the various marketing specialisms such as technology, data and commerce. And then they can steer the organization, knowing the gaps that need to be filled, either internally or externally.

---

3 Process: *To Simplify and Speed-up*

To become healthier, companies need to *blow-up* rigid, cumbersome organizational processes. This will often require a reorganization, for example, a merging of teams and disciplines.

It is rare that a process can be changed without some form of impact on the people that carry out the process and how they all connect with each other. That is why it is often good to have an external consultant to come in and help.

The focus must be on simplicity. With that will come increased efficiency. And, therefore, speed.

An additional element to add to this is collaboration. In a post-pandemic world, where we are more likely working remotely from each other, creating a connected workforce is more important than ever. As part of the process companies must think about how technology can be used to bring everyone together into a connected ecosystem. One that is enriching, and also creates the bond between the organization and the individual.

4

Insight: *Unlock Commercial Value of Data*

A 2020 study by McKinsey found that 58 percent of consumer interactions with businesses were digital. That is why companies are awash with data. Often hidden within this data are complex patterns of behavior that, if understood and executed upon, could provide tremendous commercial value.

In order to reach a healthier state, the focus must be on consolidating and connecting all data sources together into one unified view, and then connecting this into platforms that touch the consumer. For lower-funnel activity, this could enable the creation of a closed loop—where the action and the results are linked together in a self-optimizing system into which machine learning can be placed to take over the decision. In this evolved state, the role of the human is less in the area of execution and more in the area of interpretation: steering and shaping.

5

Measurement: *To Align Everyone*

We have more to measure than ever before, and not all of it matters. The author William Cameron describes it thus: "Not everything that can be counted counts. Not everything that counts can be counted." As we have discussed in the previous two chapters, the hypnotic effects of measurable data have distracted us from what really matters—what really drives the business. Therefore, on top of the closed-loop system that is optimizing the lower-funnel activity we need to build an additional layer that captures the long-term effects. And then to have one all-encompassing KPI. A compound KPI that can unify everything.

Dr. Katie Best of the London School of Economics says that very few companies have found this compound KPI. "Companies get it really wrong and end up with loads of different areas of measurement on their scorecards. It should be really elegant and simple." Polly Cochrane underscores this point, with the importance of connecting everything together: "We need to become better at explaining the alchemy that is optimized marketing. It's not just about joining the 'paid, owned, earned' dots but considering them all at the same time, understanding the impact each has on the others and knowing how and when to pull each lever to make a whole thing hum."

All organizations need a holistic approach to measurement that captures the interdependencies between hard and soft measures of marketing and then allow the reporting to help improve the functioning of the company. Anna Suchopar, General Counsel & Company Secretary at ASOS, reinforced how reporting was used to improve the teams and remove barriers: "We put a new organizational reporting process in place, which provides us with visibility on the roadblocks that we are facing."

Building for the future.

Let us imagine that the foundations are largely optimized. And that there is a good state of health. From this strong foundational position, the company can start to go further and begin to imagine a new structure for the future, based on the nature of the type of organization that it is. That is what we are going to explore now. And it starts with understanding the type of organization you are within.

Identifying Your Organizational Type

There are many ways of clustering organizations in types. The one we are going to use is based on two dimensions that will ultimately cluster all companies into one of four types.

The dimensions we are going to use are as follows:

1 *Product-led versus Marketing-led*

Does the business focus on the product or is the focus on the ever-changing nature of the market?

2. *Centralized or Decentralized*

To what extent is the organization controlled from the center and/or a central unit versus devolved to a market and/or various departments?

NB: Companies will sit somewhere between these axes, not always sitting completely in one quadrant. However, forcing one to decide can provide a level of clarity—as the intent is simply to provoke thinking, not to present the answers.

These questions help pinpoint the organizational identity—where does your company sit?

The Organizational Identity Matrix

CENTRALIZED

PRODUCT-LED

MARKETING-LED

THE FOUR IDENTITY QUADRANTS

Engineers Highly engineered organizations that are centered on product excellence and consistency of delivery *Think:* Apple, Dyson, LG, Volkswagen, Uber	**Networkers** Highly networked organizations of specialists working together to constantly evolve the product based on market conditions *Think:* Airbnb, HSBC, Verizon, Diageo
Inventors Highly inventive organizations that adapt products and marketing relevant to each market *Think:* Google, Zoom, DropBox, Slack	**Entrepreneurs** Highly entrepreneurial organizations responding to marketing conditions with a diverse product and marketing output *Think:* Universal Music, easyJet, Flutter (e.g. Fox Bet)

DECENTRALIZED

NB: Some large multinational companies may not sit squarely in one of the four quadrants. This is mostly due to the fact that each of the different divisions need to be considered individually. For example, for Unilever, Food and Refreshment would have the characteristic of a Networker, where there is a lot of local market insight impacting product development and marketing. If you are struggling to assign the company to a quadrant, try assessing at a division level.

Clearly, each of the four types would need to prioritize different areas when thinking about how to set up their marketing, including the technology and talent that they need, where it resides and how it connects together. Let's unpack them—starting with the Engineers.

Engineers

What are they?

Highly engineered organizations that are centered on product excellence and consistency of delivery.

Think: Apple, Dyson, LG, Uber, Volkswagen.

The role of marketing

Engineer-based organizations typically have a product schedule that is clear and ordered. Marketing will have a line of sight on what is coming down the pipe and will need to respond, finding a market for the product. The centralized nature of the Engineer organization is often seen in the way that assets are created; centrally created and often with a greater amount of time allowed for crafting.

Having an unchanging creative oversight is important—whether within the organization or outsourced—so that the branding remains consistent. With the average tenure of a Marketing Director being three years, it is important that Engineer organizations build creative direction that can last many years, perhaps decades. Agencies then provide fresh interpretations of the core theme for each new campaign based on what is happening in culture.

What about global?

With the global Engineer organizations, the product/service is likely to be similar across markets, therefore, a lot of the production of assets and the execution of media can be done centrally or within hubs. This can include programmatic buying and paid social, with local markets curating the inventory that is bought by the hubs.

Local markets are responsible for executing analog channels and also media environments that require a more editorial style of execution: local content, media partnerships, influencer marketing, etc.

The centralizing of execution into hubs provides efficiency and also consistency, but still allows local markets to shape the campaign so it is culturally relevant.

Inventors:

What are they?

Highly inventive organizations that adapt products and marketing relevant to each market.

Think: Google, Zoom, DropBox, Slack.

The role of marketing

Inventor-based organizations are different from Engineering-based organizations in that they have a less centralized structure. This often frees up a range of marketers, and marketing agencies, to produce a broad array of different activities ranging from CRM, paid communications, branded content, influencer marketing, events, brand partnerships and sponsorship. This enables a rich tapestry of communication. In order to establish some form of control over this, the Inventor organization needs to have a consistent brand positioning and a business KPI that all parties work to; with a specific marketing KPI for each marketing strand based on its role within the marketing funnel. The Inventor organization needs to seek out and attract the most creative and pioneering agency partners within their country. To constantly be pushing the boundaries.

What about global?

The global Inventor organization must put in place a capability for connecting all of its markets together to enable the sharing of work and best practice. This will enable the organization to learn from itself.

On top of this, investment must be made in the training and development of marketing capability across the world.

The flexibility markets possess to do their own thing must be counterbalanced with a minimum expectation on the marketing capability that each market has built in. Agencies should support Inventor organizations with best in class expertise locally, and global leadership to help elevate the capability across markets.

Networkers

What are they?

Highly networked organizations of specialists working together to constantly evolve the product based on market conditions.

Think: Airbnb, HSBC, Verizon, Diageo.

The role of marketing

The Networker organizations are often very large and/or very mature and have become increasingly more centralized over time. Yet, they still have to respond to the changing nature of the consumer with constant refinements to the product and/or the marketing. As the name suggests this organization needs to build a highly-connected workforce that understands, and is able to operate effectively within the various areas of the business. A major focus for marketing is on finding the balance between the short-term (and being responsive to a changing marketplace) whilst keeping an eye on the long-term contribution of brand.

For many Networker organizations there is also the issue of multiple products/services creating their own clutter, with campaigns for these overlapping. Agencies can often provide real value with more holistic portfolio-based planning services that can bring some order to the activity.

What about global?

Global Networker organizations will, most likely, require most of their marketing services to be local due to the changing and nuanced nature of the marketplace. However, these organizations tend to have a significant requirement for mid and lower funnel marketing capabilities, which require advanced capability. Agencies should seek to improve the efficiency of the model by hubbing advanced services that can support the local agency teams, such as audience creation and predictive analytics. Local markets can tap into the hubs as if they are simply an extension of their own local teams.

Further efficiencies can be gained by offshoring routine services, such as ad operations and dashboard maintenance, to markets with a lower cost per employee.

Entrepreneurs

What are they?

Highly entrepreneurial organizations responding to marketing conditions with a diverse product and marketing output.

Think: Universal Music, easyJet, Flutter.

The role of marketing

Entrepreneur organizations are often dynamic places to work, in that the conditions are constantly changing, and the business needs to react fast. The single-minded focus is on the marketplace and responding fast to opportunity as it presents itself. The decentralized set up is, for many, essential in order to allow the complete freedom to be able to act fast.

This organization type has a justification for in-housing *some* executional functions if they need to be able to remove the time between the identification of an opportunity and the action. For example, a music label that spots a trend popping on social media and wants to respond very quickly with a recut music video pushed out through organic social channels. External agency support needs to be fully committed to the organization so that they are always available, perhaps even embedded within.

What about global?

For many organizations of this type each local market will be its own isolated marketplace. Therefore, the role for global is often very limited. However, as marketing services continue to evolve and become more specialized, there is value in the definition and development of marketing techniques that can be carried out locally.

And as with the Inventor organization, global leadership should also share best practice but with a greater focus on the use of technology. This can enable *real-time sharing* of trends that are popping and innovative activities that are happening at that moment, from countries across the world.

Hopefully the identity quadrant provides a more nuanced view as to how organizations can evolve. An important part of this is how to think about the relationship between in-house and outsourced talent. And how they work together. Let's take a look at that now.

In-Housing and Outsourcing.

To companies that sit within any of the four quadrants there is, and will continue to be, consideration for in-housing certain marketing functions.

With much debate about clients in-housing agency services it may seem odd that as an agency we are advocating this. However, our recommendation is the in-housing of leadership functions and not necessarily practitioner/executional functions, although more on that later.

Leadership functions have been housed within client organizations for many years now, namely roles such as Head of Media, Head of Communications, etc. These have been essential for most organizations as they provide the specialist agencies with the bandwidth to be able to communicate with the organization. The CMO or Marketing Director cannot, and does not have time to oversee the broad sweeping scope of marketing services required effectively.

As marketing services proliferate so will the need for additional in-house leadership functions. Depending on the type of organization, it is most likely that a leadership function is required to oversee the following areas: marketing, media, data, analytics, technology, website, CRM, social/community management, commerce and communications. Over time many of these individual areas will separate into more specialist areas and the importance of them will differ for each organization. For many, multiple functions will be rolled up under one individual and/or team.

The defining, scoping and hiring for this leadership talent requires a significant focus and investment—and must always be the priority focus before considering building additional capability in-house (and more on that in Chapter 4).

Beyond leadership, in-housing additional marketing capability

The question now is whether there is a commercial case to be made for in-housing beyond the leadership roles, building practitioner- and execution-based functions.

It is within the power of the marketing organization to set up its relationship with its agency partners to deliver many of the benefits that could ultimately be achieved through in-housing; namely:

Understanding: Fully dedicated teams, enabling category and business understanding/expertise. This can also include agency teams embedded into client organization.

Control: Leadership function within marketing organization to manage the work streams of the agency teams. Connected to this, live dashboards that report on marketing performance.

Transparency: Fully-disclosed and externally auditable requirements written into the contracts.

Price: Cost paid on clearly defined team with fully disclosed overhead and profit margin.

For organizations that do want to move in the direction of in-housing marketing capabilities there are, of course, many issues to work through.

Making the case, internally, for additional head count is only the beginning. There is also the need to constantly justify this investment. There is also the consideration of finding and hiring the talent, which is an additional burden on an organization. And then replacing talent as it churns. The organization needs to be able to attract talent relatively easily otherwise this becomes an ongoing issue.

However, a larger issue is on managing the talent. The marketing world is increasing in complexity and keeping pace with the change is commercially critical. Outsourced agency teams that are exposed to other experts and other clients may bring new techniques that would not necessarily be the case if in-housed.

A Client Experience of In-Housing Media.

Category: Healthcare

In-housing is not for the faint of heart and frankly not something that everyone can—and more importantly should—try and pull off. In many cases you can achieve what you need by reorganizing the relationship with your agency partners; do not underestimate the level of control you have to completely restructure the relationship. However, this may not be the right answer for some organizations—I know that was the case for me. If you do opt to in-house, these are the things that you will face. Things that I either had to really think about, or wish I was more mindful of, before I started:

1. **Efficiency or Effectiveness?** Obviously, your answer will be *both*. But be ruthlessly honest with yourself on what is the priority here. If it is the former it may be harder to achieve than initially viewed—media and platform savings may not materialize and will therefore hinder your ability to create a self-funded model. If it is the latter, be clear on how you are going to track and optimize performance over time, when the benchmark of the current agency's performance may no longer be a realistic point of comparison. Being able to answer these questions to the board will be a new, and for some organizations, heavy responsibility.

2

Selling-in and Maintaining Headcount. Making the case to build a unit may actually be a lot easier than you think, businesses like the idea of cost savings. The harder, ongoing, part will be continually justifying the headcount, particularly for businesses that are looking to maximize profit, and cut costs.

3

Attracting the Best Talent? Attracting talent is the most important focus for an agency, everything they do is to make themselves a magnet so that they have the pick of the very best. The question is how magnetic are you for the best talent—in terms of the company brand, career progression, access to other talent, training and even office location? This is fundamentally important as even a 30 percent saving on average staff cost is a rounding error when considered against the overall revenue of the organization. And yet one optimized plan could deliver 50 percent greater return than an unoptimized plan, contributing multiple millions of dollars of incremental value each year. *This is even more of an issue if your competitors do have access to top talent—even if through an agency—as this could ultimately flow through to unnecessary reductions in share of market.*

4 **Managing Talent.** Managing people's career ambitions is an important consideration. They cannot necessarily move up a hierarchy in the same way that they can within an agency. Consider how they could move within the organization. Lean on your agency partners for helping to continue to train, develop and support the talent so they are not cut off and, therefore, deskilled over time.

5 **Understand the Uncertainty and Risks?** Any mistakes that were previously owned by the agency now have to be dealt with by the organization. Financial commitments that are not met, misbooking issues and/or payment issues have to be absorbed by the organization. This will become more of an issue with increasingly restrictive data privacy regulations. Preparing the organization for this is important.

Bring the agency in on the journey. Work with them to help overcome some of the five areas of focus. A transparent model with the agency will provide more neutral advice than any tied-technology company that ultimately wants to sell you into their platform and/or data. Working with the agency to become a support function, enabling them to grow revenue with additional services that they could provide, as long as they can contribute to the business.■

But, perhaps, the biggest issue of all is the overall *commercial performance* of the collective in-house team versus an agency. For many clients they will experience a much more responsive unit in the form of an outsourced agency that is always under threat of losing a very large contract. Where they can insist that people are removed from the business and new talent brought in immediately. Without having to worry about employment constraints.

And the entire agency can be replaced every three to five years as part of a pitch process; significantly increasing the evolutionary development of that function. The high levels of competition between agencies as they tender for the client's business helps insure the most advanced capabilities are always known and, if chosen, incorporated. This is particularly important for marketing functions that are still evolving. The commercial cost of losing pace with one's competitors, in order to reduce costs, is an important consideration for in-housing■

Agency as a Platform■

Some organizations will still just want to take the functions in-house. This can often be the case for businesses that have very specialist product categories, where the emphasis on product knowledge is as, if not more, important than the marketing communication expertise. Ian Mundorff, Global Head of Media at HP cited this as one particularly important factor for in-housing: "Getting a company that is focused on acquiring micro-processors, screens and chemicals for ink cartridges to start thinking about buying media is extraordinarily difficult—that was a big uphill battle…but once we'd actually addressed it…that actually created a lot more speed within the system."

However, for other companies the motivation to in-house maybe for other reasons; the psychological dimension of business cannot be ignored, as the sense of ownership of one's own destiny is a very powerful motivator for many people within business. And it must be respected, and supported.

Whatever the reason, in this situation, the agency's role needs to evolve to that of a platform; to provide a range of wraparound services to help the marketing organization on its journey.

As Mundorff says: "In this new model we view our agency as an important strategic partner providing specific skills that we know that we cannot replicate in-house—also to be able to understand what's happening in the industry and amongst our peer set."

"We view our agency as an important strategic partner providing specific skills that we know that we cannot replicate in-house."

Ian Mundorff,
Global Head of Media at HP

This can start with provision of talent, training and replenishment.

Mundorff cites strategy as an important outsourced capability. "There are strategic elements that we can't replicate, - even the role of comms planning—that is not a capability that I currently have within my organization. The flexibility provided by the agency remains critical for us and allows me to be able to say, 'we've got a project, I need your best comms planner'."

Additionally, an agency can provide support for the more advanced capabilities such as data scientists that can create bespoke algorithms or dynamic creative optimization planners for building complex decision trees within a DSP. For both strategic and advanced capabilities, the talent is often harder to find and more readily available within an agency.

For media and technology agencies, specifically, providing services such as the negotiation of contracts with major tech vendors and the curation of inventory, the agency holding companies can bring the benefits of scale. Negotiating reduced rates and then buying through a programmatic platform to get the additional benefits of the targeting filter. As Scott Hagedorn says: "There is a misconception that there's no way to create clout in the programmatic world. [Agencies] can use the technology to decision the banks of inventory that we have taken a longer-term position on."

One thing for sure is that the role of the agency will continue to change as clients' needs change. And we will explore this a bit further in Chapter 5. For now, let's take a moment to take stock and process what we have just covered.

"For clients that do want to in-house there are opportunities for holding companies to become a Value-Added Reseller (VAR), a reseller of multiple Cloud solutions and then to provide services on top of that."

Scott Hagedorn
CEO of OMG North America

Organizational Re-think | 5 Steps.

1. Carry out an internal audit of the marketing competency against the five key fundamentals to assess current state of foundational health

2. Create taskforce for each of the five—to improve each area

3. Optimize the organizational structure—plot the organizational type on the identity matrix to prioritize how to evolve the structure and type of capability for the future

4. Create a roadmap to achieve new model—workshopped with key stakeholders

5. Create a separate resource to lead the change—with key milestones to report back to the wider business

Taking Stock.

As we move beyond the marketing midlife crisis into a healthier state of being we need to make sure that we upgrade the foundations. This will ensure that the technology, capability, processes, insight and measurement are all fully optimized.

And from this, start to think about how to structure the organization for the future, considering the type of organization, from Engineer, Inventor, through to Networker or Entrepreneur. Each of the four has a very different requirement for marketing. And, therefore, a very different requirement for the capabilities, structure and ways of working.

As part of this, consider the skills that need to be brought within the marketing organization, with a priority on leadership roles covering the increasingly more specialist array of marketing services; essential to create the bandwidth between client organization and agencies.

And for organizations that do want to in-house practitioner and executional capabilities, agencies need to think about the services that they can wraparound them to help support them on their endeavor. This changes the nature of the agency to that of a platform service.

This ultimately hints at the future of the agency: one that is more modular in nature; adaptable to the change in conditions of the client and the marketplace. And perhaps with a decentralized workforce of expertise. All of which comes with serious implications for how we manage our talent.

Something that we are going to look at now.

Chapter 4

A People-Future

04

Shaped

So far, *Shift* has explored the complexity of the modern marketing landscape and described the resulting midlife crisis impacting the marketing community as it navigates this complexity. In the previous chapter we laid the foundation of how to build for the future, but we have yet to address one of the most important elements of successfully navigating the next half decade—the people.

So much time and focus has been placed on technology and data, and not enough on talent. Of course, this does not mean the former is not important, but it has hijacked the agenda, almost completely. It is now time to rebalance; to apply the same level of advanced precision thinking to how we go about managing the multitude of minds that work within our organizations.

We are going to borrow from the gurus of personal development to help us explore how marketing organizations can evolve to become true people-centric organizations. The three fundamental steps to personal development start with understanding oneself. From this deeper understanding comes clarity on one's reason for purpose. And finally, the habits that need to be cultivated to achieve the purpose. Let's start by looking deep within—to know thyself. Or, at least, the organization's self.

Know Thyself
Find One's Purpose
Cultivate New Habits

Our Three Steps to Personal Development:

Know Thyself.

Clearly any successful business has always focused on the ultimate endpoint of growth. This will always be the overriding priority to be balanced with the psychological and spiritual development of its employees. However, the single-minded focus on the former without an understanding on the contribution of the latter is a mistake that many organizations continue to make.

The focus towards the former is more likely to happen as technology and data rises up the corporate agenda. This is the phenomenon that we have witnessed in marketing over the last five to 10 years; and with it, we have seen a people-shaped hole emerge in the marketing industry. This further compounds an innate view within most organizations that talent is a *cost* to the organization, rather than an ongoing and critical investment that must be made to grow the business.

Nancy F. Koehn of the Harvard Business School observes that: "One of the things we want to unpack is the idea that your people aren't your most important investment; and getting the right people, keeping them with you, keeping them challenged, pushing them harder and making them feel incredibly engaged and inspired to do that work, is the work of the firm. The essential work of the firm, because that's what delivers back the service profit and that's what delivers money and a reason to be."

When talent is seen purely as a cost, it is naturally reduced to the bare minimum

Marketing-based businesses have become so accustomed to stripped-back efficiency as the assumed stance, that there is little slack left for the vital role of innovative and creative thinking at the best of times, let alone in a crisis. As Koehn sees it: "We've spent 15 years developing no slack whatsoever in any system of a company—the people system, the supply system, the information provision and distribution system—no slack. Let's get it all out, let's be lean and mean. Well, that doesn't work so well when disaster strikes, or a crisis strikes or turbulence ratchets from high level to a red-hot previously unperceived level and a level we haven't yet experienced. You actually need to start thinking."

Stripped-back efficiency, coupled with employees feeling overwhelmed and overworked has led to fatigue creeping in and individuals feeling a lack of control and, in some cases, detachment from their jobs.

Work, worth doing

For many, day-to-day roles have become reduced to a series of tasks to be done: we are servicing the platforms, processes and tools with which we all work. From campaign reporting to presentation writing and executive summarizing of our efforts—we are engaged more in repeatable, replicable tasks than we are in the more human endeavor of using our curiosity, creativity and courage to drive game-changing solutions and disproportionate outcomes. As we shift into the future of marketing, how can we place renewed effort on identifying and focusing on the work that is worth doing, and swiftly jettisoning everything and anything else?

Further compounding these issues is the observation that the career, in the conventional sense, is a very particular construct of the second half of the 20th century, and one that many believe is no longer fit for purpose. Bruce Daisley, author of *The Joy of Work*, observes that in many modern marketing organizations, there is a fixed promotion grid that acts a little like a conveyor belt. You can only get promoted every two years. The academic assessment of forced rankings—used by many marketing organizations—is not generally positive and is associated with demotivated workers and performance.

Becoming a Firm of Endearment

In their seminal book *Firms of Endearment*, authors Raj Sisodia, David B. Wolfe and Jag Sheth describe how in developed markets, many employees are looking for more than a pay check from their work; they want "psychic income" as well as monetary income. They observed that employees are looking for work that engages the whole person, fulfills social needs and is meaningful and psychologically rewarding. In short, people want to view their work as a calling.

Their analysis of companies that delivered on this need found that such organizations could not only afford to be highly selective in employee recruitment because they are attractive places to work, but that these companies outperformed the market in terms of shareholder returns by significant orders of magnitude. In fact, over a 10-year period, *Firms of Endearment* companies outperformed even *Good to Great* companies by three to one).

And yet there is so much evidence to support the commercial case for investing in talent.

Investing in people is an investment that can pay back in dividends, both to employees and the future of the organization. Creating a culture of employee development will lead to enhanced retention rates and will inevitably attract new talent to the business. Increased motivation and collaboration create better, stronger customer service. Your employees are your greatest asset—and their success drives client outcomes—so it is important that you keep them engaged, challenged, and supported.

As the world recovers from the global pandemic, organizations will have to think again about how they manage talent. Expectations of more flexibility and independence will have increased. Organizations that enable this will attract better talent than their competitors and are likely to grow ahead of them. However, it will take more than the commitment of a couple of days working from home. Organizations need to use this moment to rethink the nature of how they bring people together and motivate them toward a collective effort. This starts with clarity on what exactly the collective effort is. Time to move onto the second of the three steps.

Know Thyself

1 Assess current health of the business

2 Benchmark against similar organizations

3 Create strategic talent agenda

Find One's Purpose.

This step is about establishing what it is that your organization is aiming to achieve beyond profit. Your purpose, contends Nancy F. Koehn, is who you are. "That's what purpose ultimately is. It's an identifier, it's a statement of identity. I don't think that's going to cease. I think it's going to get greater and greater."

It has been argued that emerging generations draw identity from their organizations to a greater extent than previous generations. And that purpose of the organization is a significant factor alongside salary when deciding where to work.

So yes, purpose and mission has never been more important. But Koehn reinforces that it must be authentic. "It's got to be real, because radical transparency will find it out quickly, and you'll be worse off than you were before you cooked up the kind of fake purpose statement."

The senior leadership of any organization must identify the inner motivation that drove the foundation of the company. Beyond revenue it will be there, albeit sometimes very faint. From that, the purpose can be identified and materialized. Creating a filter and focus, and a collective endeavor, to guide the organization into the future. From the types of products and services it creates, through to how it communicates these.

And to be clear, although identifying the purpose may be an effective organizational prerequisite for aligning and motivating, it does not mean that it needs to be communicated to consumers. In fact, if the motivation for defining the purpose is ultimately so that it can be used for marketing purposes with consumers, it is likely to have the opposite effect internally as it strips away any semblance of authenticity.

A tool to craft organizational purpose.

PHD, working with eatbigfish, released two books on challenger thinking: *Overthrow* and *Overthrow II*. The books present a framework from which organizations can define the challenge they are seeking to overcome in the world or within their own category. The challenger archetypes are summarized at the back of this book and can be explored further at: www.phdmedia.com/overthrow

Higher-order purpose

The vast majority of businesses do not need to save the world. They do, however, need to be clear about their intent. That is enough. However, if the organization has a higher-order purpose that ultimately seeks to positively impact something outside of its own direct benefit—this should obviously be used as the clearly stated motivation to galvanize all employees. As long as it is authentic and core to the functioning nature of the business. If it is ancillary, then it should not be the focus.

Higher-order purposes could range from seeking to affect perception and behavior change in the population through to instigating policy change at a governmental level. This puts the company in the service of the greater good and is a very compelling motivational driver for talent; it is achieving something remarkable in the world.

And in some cases, there is great dividend in communicating this externally to consumers. The contribution this may have to return on investment should be taken into consideration, and the impact it could have internally on individuals within the organization. Unilever's Conny Braams, identifies this as an important contribution that the agency can make. "Our agency partners have an exciting challenge to help our brands take action on the matters people care about. From ensuring progressive portrayals of people in our advertising, which we know is the right thing to do for society and it increases purchase intent, to putting purpose at the heart of a brand's proposition. Actioning this with ambition, aiming for fame." In particular making sure that the *commercial* case for this type of investment is made, "ensuring a continued and sustained focus on increased effectiveness and efficiency."

Once the organization is clear about its purpose, it can start to develop the habits to help achieve it, beginning with how it manages its employees.■

Find One's Purpose.

1 Workshops to define an organization's reason for existing, beyond revenue. Think identity, product, culture, values and motivational drivers for talent

2 Include all important stakeholders. And seek the view of the organization at large

3 State it clearly and simply. Transparency is key

4 Bring it to life and live it every day

Cultivate New Habits.

Although each organization will develop its own habits bespoke to its purpose, there are some foundational habits that need to be put in place to optimize talent management.

Habit #1: Hire for Tomorrow

At the most fundamental level, the three components that make for remarkable individuals within marketing are: curiosity, cognitive ability and clarity of mind. These will continue to be the key criteria for marketing talent. Marketing roles will increasingly become more heterogeneous, specializing into further areas of technical sophistication.

Jeffrey F. Rayport of Harvard Business School predicts that we will see a wide range of new specializations emerge. He believes that in marketing, as in so many fields, we will need to put a premium on recruiting *T-shaped* people. These are individuals who are highly skilled generalists but also possess a deep vertical specialization. Given the complexity of our field, Rayport explains, that we really need *π-shaped* people—skilled generalists with two or more deep verticals.

There is also going to be an increasing need for people to work with machine learning. Or, more specifically, algorithms. That will require individuals that have *Stempathy*, a phrase coined by Thomas Friedman, the American political commentator and author. According to Friedman, *Stempathy* jobs combine STEM (science, technology, engineering, math) skills with human empathy. Friedman wrote: "Leaders, businesses and communities will still leverage technology to gain advantage, but those that put human connection at the center of everything they do—and how they do it—will be the enduring winners."

"Machines can be programmed to do the next thing right. But only humans can do the next right thing."

Thomas Friedman.

Rayport agrees: "We can offload lots of *interoperability* and quantitative analysis to machines, but the people who manage them still need to understand what's going on—and to integrate that with the human, consumer, creative, and narrative aspects of marketing. I don't believe it's enough to say that we'll have a division of labor between people and machines without also saying that integration will become increasingly important. Human talent will put these two sides of human and machine capabilities together, especially in the context of those very human interactions called relationships which we all must manage."

The next generation of employees will need to be capable in anticipating bias in algorithms, generating genuine behavioral insight from data, and improving on the recommended outcome or optimization.

It's time to stop sleeping.

Finding and attracting the talent of the future should be keeping business leaders awake at night

Not all businesses can be coveted as the hottest place to work so, unless you can afford to overpay the market rate, a different approach to attracting, retaining and developing this talent in marketing organizations will be required. Marketing organizations, working in close connection with the agencies, should be planning for the future. A strategy to hire the next generation talent base is opening up the filter on where they hire from.

Apprentices, recruitment and training specialist Multiverse notes that most marketing organizations are still sticking to the status quo of graduate schemes for early talent, instead of thinking about reaching and developing talent through alternative entry routes, where the recruitment strategy is still based on prior academic attainment, rather than future potential.

Multiverse believes organizations should start challenging themselves on whether their academic entry requirements correlate to job performance or, again, if this is simply the *status quo* that has gone unchallenged.

Multiverse has worked with employers to deliver some best-in-class approaches with organizations using contextualized recruitment with great results; where employers can really understand an applicant's achievements in the context in which they are achieved, and understand the systematic barriers an applicant may have had to overcome. These best-in-class examples are achieved when outreach and community partnerships work closely with the recruitment teams in organizations.

And, of course, to best ensure a marketing organization's recruitment strategy is credible and authentic, it needs to ensure inclusion is embedded into the organization's DNA.

Bringing in talent from a diversity of backgrounds through hiring is just one part of inclusion. Companies must work to also ensure they have inclusive teams and management to create a sense of belonging and psychological safety for all employees to contribute.

With more and more organizations embarking on diversity programs, it is essential to understand what that truly means and the benefits that a diverse workforce can have on a company's performance. The success of any DE&I program hinges on demonstrating impact across the talent lifecycle—from sourcing and hiring through succession and separation.

McKinsey's 2015 Diversity Matters Report states: "More diverse companies, we believe, are better able to win top talent and improve their customer orientation, employee satisfaction, and decision making, and all that leads to a virtuous cycle of increasing returns. This, in turn, suggests that other kinds of diversity—for example, in age, sexual orientation, and experience (such as a global mind-set and cultural fluency)—are also likely to bring some level of competitive advantage for companies that can attract and retain such diverse talent."

However, it is not just about getting a diverse population through the doors. A 2017 Forbes study revealed that diversity must be followed up with inclusivity at all levels of decision-making to maximize business performance. Results showed:

- Inclusive teams make better business decisions up to 87 percent of the time.
- Teams that follow an inclusive process make decisions twice as fast with half the meetings.
- Decisions made and executed by diverse teams delivered 60 percent better results[1].

[1] *https://www.forbes.com/sites/forbescoachescouncil/2019/09/09/the-benefits-of-creating-a-diverse-workforce/*

Habit #2: Help people get clarity on their innate strengths

It is crucial to build a deep organizational understanding into the nature of how people's minds actually work and encourage them to focus on different specialist areas based on their most distinctive and differentiated contribution. Whether it is precision thinking, lateral thinking, or an aptitude for emotional intelligence, this is about getting people into the right swim lanes and, in doing so, enabling them to thrive. Understanding innate strengths and weaknesses can also assist when creating learning pathways for employees.

A growing number of prominent companies have reformed their approach to recruitment processes to factor in a greater understanding of people's innate strengths; among them are Hewlett Packard Enterprise, Microsoft and Ford. Many others including Dell, IBM and Deloitte have either started up such initiatives or have exploratory efforts under way. They are claiming that the programs are already paying off in ways far beyond reputational enhancement: in employee engagement, innovation and increased productivity.

What's your innate strength?

Ceri Ellis—a specialist learning expert—helped PHD develop a categorization of the different innate strengths and the types of roles employees are most suited to in any organization. See if you can recognize yourself or anyone you know.

The Six Innate Strengths:

TYPE	Strength	Roles
PRECISIONISTS	**Turns Disorder into Order** Able to learn new information quickly, are precise and detail oriented, have a strong adherence to rules, a drive for perfection, intellectual curiosity and are logical thinkers.	Analytical and highly technical roles
SOLUTIONISTS	**Finds a Way Through** Likely to be highly creative, exceptional problem solvers, original thinkers and talented visualisers. They are often exceptionally gifted verbally.	Creative and strategic development roles
RESILIANTS	**Pushes On** Likely to be highly resilient, tenacious, good at problem solving with strong verbal skills and empathetic strengths.	High-pressure roles, including client and stakeholder management
LATERALISTS	**Creates the Unexpected** Original thinkers, are creative, energetic and can have high levels of perseverance when interested in a topic. An ability to laser focus when engaged.	Creative and dynamic roles, where there is constant change
CONNECTORS	**Aligns Minds** Likely to have excellent listening skills, have great strengths in oral recall and memorization They can thrive in social communication.	Stakeholder-management and internal people development
DEVELOPERS	**Frames the View** Clarity of mind, able to construct and frame a perspective with clarity and order.	Strategic- and writing-based roles

In addition, Ceri Ellis facilitated the creation of an online tool to enable people to identify the innate strengths they are more likely to have. The tool is called ISI (Innate Strengths Indicator)—a link to this can be found on www.shiftbyphd.com. This is a useful resource that can be used by individuals to help them develop a greater understanding of their inner strengths.

With our future talent well positioned in the most suitable swim lanes, the focus is now on how to create the optimal conditions to enable them to contribute at the highest level possible.

Habit #3: Set People Free (within a Framework)

In a recent interview, Arsène Wenger, Arsenal FC manager from 1996 to 2018, said that very few footballers ever achieve their full potential. Although most professional footballers have high standards, those that achieved their full potential were the ones able to more accurately assess their own performance. They did not rely on being told; they had an inner sense of self-ownership and empowerment.

Michael Leiter, a professor of industrial and organizational psychology at Victoria's Deakin University describes this: "People have a real need for that autonomy. And by autonomy I don't mean, 'I can do whatever I like', it's about that feeling of making something happen as opposed to being acted upon."

For most people, the biggest thing missing from modern work, according to Bruce Daisley, is a sense of control. People feel helpless, that they have no control over their work.

It is not a localized problem; a Gallup survey found that only 13 percent of workers are globally engaged in their jobs, and that over half of all workers are disengaged with their jobs. It gets worse. Around 20 percent of workers are actively disengaged—these people are more likely to be engaged in actively bringing down their organization, rather than being supporters of it.

Daisley argues there is evidence that the more control we have over our situation, the more we can do things that we did not believe possible. You can keep going when you feel you are electing to do it. When there is a feeling you have an impact on something, you get greater levels of lean in. Interestingly, you do not need to give people a lot of control for them to feel motivated again.

This was also the conclusion of research carried out by David H. Maister, professor at the Harvard Business School and author of *Practice What You Preach*. His research tracked 139 offices, from 29 professional service firms in 15 countries, and in 15 different lines of business. It stripped out acquisitional growth to focus solely on organic growth. The model tracked the different styles of management and the impact on organic growth.

The three most significant management styles that led to dramatic uplifts in organic growth were: high standard, empowerment and coaching. When all three are applied at the same time you get lift off. Put simply, create a stretch goal with the individual, allow them to work out how they are going to achieve it and be there for them as a coach to help them achieve it.

Although it is important that the line manager performs the role of the coach, there are significant benefits in building a coaching infrastructure, which includes reverse-mentoring and peer-to-peer learning partnerships that provide ongoing stimulation, the self-motivation to learn more, as well as building trust and emotional bonds.

Some organizations have gone further and created a freedom-of-movement structure in which people rotate from one department to another. The aim of this is not only to acquire more experience of the business, but to also develop a network of relationships in different departments. This will help faster resolution of problems or challenges in the business.

Technology can play a role here in reimagining the workflow of the day-to-day, particularly technologies that have been designed in a way that functions like games. Game design can create highly immersive work experiences. Where any action results in an immediate response. And as one improves their contribution, they see their performance increase. With a social layer for acknowledgement and reinforcement. With the ultimate aim of creating a *flow-state*. Arguably game design is more important as people work remotely. Keeping them connected and immersed.

It can help foster the final of the four habits, which may just be the most important of all.

Habit #4: Become a Learning Institution

Students walking into university or college will have a very different feeling inside compared to those individuals walking into a business. The former will have an innate sense that the agenda is about them. About them taking in new information or learning new skills. The latter will feel that it is about the company. About servicing the company's agenda. That they are trading youth for money.

It is surely within the potential of human imagination to reconfigure the organizational workflow of a company to place the employee at the center, where their focus on personal development is inextricably linked to the revenue growth of the organization. The servicing of a client or internal stakeholder's needs are part of the apparatus they use for working on their own skill set.

If, and only if, the operating model can be structured so this focus is aligned to revenue growth, it should be a serious consideration as we move into the future. It would resonate with next generations; attracting and retaining better talent and, crucially, enablingthem to unleash more potential.

Nancy F. Koehn sees this as vital for the future: "For younger people and older employees or talent, it's about 'my journey' and 'myself as I grow, as I change'. It's about, 'right, how does the firm regard that project of mine, that self-making project?'"

Building a Learning Culture that Connects

Building a learning culture is arguably more important now as we move to a more balanced work/home set up. If 2020 taught us anything, it is the power for Learning and Development (L&D) programs to give back, to support an employee as they manage their way through change and give them a sense of control. It can also build a sense of commonality across geographies and a sense of community.

These things were always there, but they are more intensified during times of change, and the value more apparent. As organizations move to a hybrid office/work from home model, this unique value proposition of L&D will continue to flex its weight, allowing the L&D teams to quantify the business impact of this emotional support and allow it to drive some of their business decisions.

The work from home reality that many of us experienced in 2020 shone a spotlight on the important business impact that can be delivered by L&D; specifically its ability to deliver against the emotional needs of employees, and the need to stay connected as a community and gain a sense of control during a time of great change.

Learning to Evolve

As marketing becomes more specialized, L&D becomes more important. Ten years ago, the industry talked about the digital divide—companies were populated by digital natives and digital immigrants. Going forward we will see many new *divides* as the discipline of marketing evolves.

Learning is a commitment that often eats into free time. But it is one that is essential. Those that invest will evolve along with the needs of the business. As Marina Gorbis, Executive Director of the Institute of the Future, has observed: "The big divide will be the 'motivational divide'; who has the self-motivation, grit and persistence to take advantage of all the free or online tools to create, collaborate, and continue learning."

If individuals want to have currency in the marketplace in the future and compete for the best jobs in the new normal, they will need to organize themselves to adapt quickly, learn and collaborate while constantly prioritizing new skills. This has huge implications for what we learn, and how we learn it, throughout the course of our marketing careers.

Removing gaps between learning and application

The most important trend in education, according to Multiverse's Inclusion and Diversity Lead Siobhan Randell, is the development of what we call *applied learning*.

Applied learning happens when the skills are embedded and remembered through immediate testing and practice in the workplace. This is how habits are formed and it is what ensures apprenticeships do not suffer from the pitfalls of most corporate training, where participants never use the things they are told and, therefore, immediately forget them. The added benefit of applied learning is that this form of learning is more suited to empowering a more diverse group of employees, who genuinely represent the societies companies seek to serve. In doing so it makes an immense contribution to equality in the workplace.

It is clear that we need to radically improve the way we train and develop people within the marketing industry. We urgently need to create and commit to new habits around how we approach the L&D of talent, equipping them for the future.

Cultivate New Habits.

1 Hire for tomorrow (increase diversity, opening the filter on the talent acquisition process)

2 Encourage greater understanding of innate strengths (enable people to get into optimal swim lanes)

3 Set people free (institutionalize a culture of empowerment and coaching)

4 Become a learning institution (that also happens to be a business). Einstein reputedly said: "Learning is experience. Everything else is just information."

Looking ahead.

The final chapter of *Shift* will focus on the future. However, there is one element of the future worth covering within this chapter about talent—the management of talent that *does not work for your organization*, or any organization. A decentralized workforce—of freelancers and hired-in talent—that is self-employed or employed by other organizations.

The workforce futurist Andy Spence believes that a "new decentralized workforce will emerge from the rubble of defunct 20th century organizational structures that will unleash the economic, and social, potential of people."

He suggests that jobs will be unbundled into discrete tasks; and in doing so, "work will be reconstituted into new forms, empowering a more diverse group of workers to reach their potential. New types of organizations, markets, platforms, and work ecosystems will evolve that are better suited for our needs in the Digital COVID Age (DC Age)."

Work, as Spence sees it, is in the process of unbundling itself. And when it rebundles it will not be on the terms or by the structures of legacy organizations, but instead through a decentralized workforce of *micropreneurs*. These include what he terms as: gig workers, slashies, playbourers, bounty hunters, livestreamers, content creators, teachers, data labourers and digital shoppers.

The *micropreneur* roles of the future▪

Futurist Andy Spence envisages a globally decentralized workforce that extends well beyond traditional concepts of jobs and organizations, and includes:

- *Gig Workers*—up to one in seven working-age adults in the US have worked via a platform at some point, in an economy that includes artists, on-call workers, contractors, seasonal workers and even a few consultants
- *Slashies*—people who work across different types of jobs to make a living—as in "I love being a writer/speaker/advisor/coach/curator/activist/slashie"
- *Playborers*—this hybrid of play and labor is found specifically in the digital games industry, where you have, for example, YouTube influencers and modders getting paid to play games

- *Bounty Hunters*—people who are motivated by a reward or prizes for completing a given task. For example, the Bounties Network[1] used tokens to incentivize the clean-up of plastic pollution in the Philippines
- *Livestreamers*—people broadcasting user-created video in real-time on gaming platforms such as Twitch, or non-gaming platforms like Caffeine for interactive shows
- *Content Creators*—it is estimated that the average creator producing comics, photographs and stories on Patreon earns around $2,000 per month, with some much more if they have a lot of patrons subscribing to high payment tiers[2]
- *Teachers*—increasingly people are able to make a living through teaching and coaching. Nearly 500 course creators on Teachable make more than $100,000 per year
- *Data Laborers*—in their book *Radical Markets*[3], Eric A. Posner and E. Glen Weyl "imagine a world in which your personal data, currently hoovered up by tech companies and repurposed for their profit, is honored as your dignified work and compensated as such." Imagine that?
- *Digital Shopkeepers*—there are millions of digital shopkeepers using platforms such as Shopify, Amazon, eBay and Etsy to keep their digital shops open all hours

[1] *https://bounties.network/*
[2] *https://www.format.com/magazine/features/art/artists-making-living-patreon*
[3] *http://radicalmarkets.com/chapters/data-as-labor/*
Source: https://workforcefuturist.substack.com/p/unleashing-the-decentralised-workforce

Spence's work with the Blockchain Research Institute envisions "a future where you would expect to see smaller companies with a highly paid cadre of contracted core workers—pulling skills from networks of teams when needed. Higher quality jobs, but less of them."

In this future-state it would be an error of judgment for leaders of companies to not consider the decentralized workforce as employees, and potentially highly valuable ones at that. This decentralized team will gravitate to the organization that has the largest emotional campfire. It will make them more committed. When they have competing demands for jobs from multiple organizations, they would choose the one they feel most connected to. That has invested in them. And their contributions were more likely to be of a higher standard.

Aside from managing remote working, managing this decentralized workforce is going to be an important requirement for the future, as we emerge from the pandemic into the mid and latter part of the 2020s.■

Summary.

After more than a decade of talking about technology and data, it is essential that the agenda now rebalances towards the most important contributor to the marketing organization—talent. We need to take an equally enlightened and advanced a pproach to how we optimize its contribution as we have done with technology.

Historically, for many organizations, when the subject of talent is raised at board level it is often not taken as seriously as the discussion of an acquisition or investment in technology. In part, this is caused by a fundamental belief system that talent is a cost, not an investment.

It is now time for us to move fully into the 21st century, and take a commercial view of talent as an investment, as a driver of growth.

This starts with an honest assessment of our organization's current approach to managing talent. And then, building a purpose-based organization that is authentic and motivating for future generations. And then, developing a range of bespoke habits to manifest the purpose—habits that include hiring for the future; assigning to swim lanes, development empowerment frameworks and creating a learning institution. And then, start to build the distributed and decentralized workforce of specialists required for the future of marketing; putting in place an infrastructure that holds them together and draws them in.

This is the most unoptimized area of scope for any senior marketing or agency leader. As we look forward, the companies that advance the way they manage their talent will most likely grow ahead of their competitors.

The remaining question is what are the specific roles we are going to need in the future? That is the subject of the next chapter.

So, let us now lift our eyes up to the horizon and attempt to do, what most organizations know better than to try and do, and predict the future roles of marketing.

Chapter 5

05

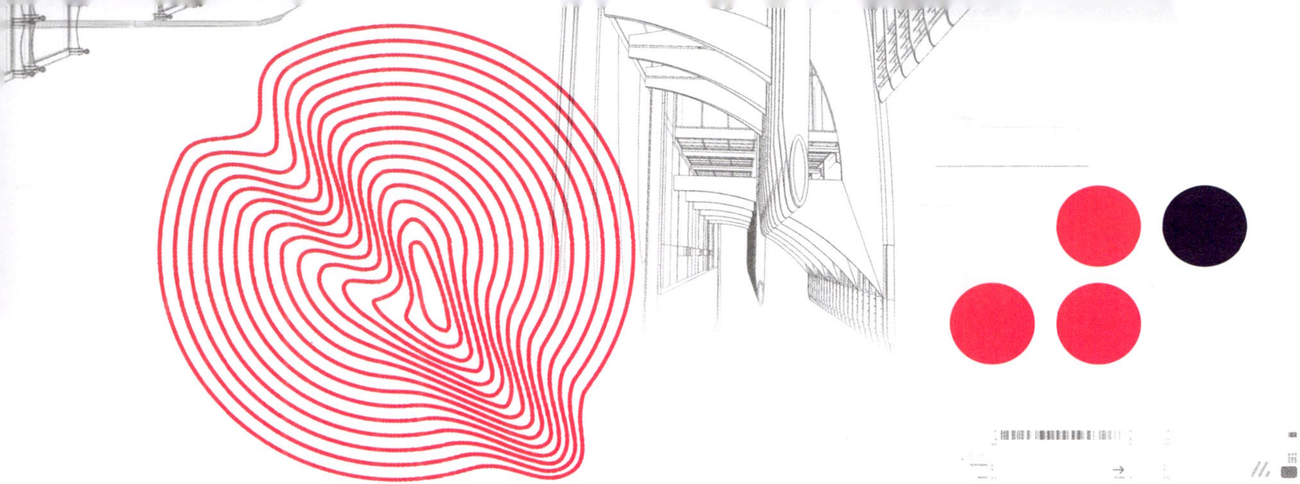

Anticipating Tomorrow.

So, to the final chapter. And to the future. Where we are going to lift our eyes up towards the horizon. And try and predict the next five to 10 years.

Now, it is worth stating that prediction is actually very easy to do. It is accurate prediction that is difficult. As Niels Bohr, the Nobel laureate in Physics and father of the atomic model, is quoted as saying: "Prediction is very difficult, especially if it's about the future." It is very easy to stray into the hyperbole, risking liquidating any credibility we may have managed to generate over the previous four chapters.

From experience the best approach is to create a logically-linked method.

That starts with a very clear understanding of the reality of the practice of marketing today. And how it is changing over time; recently witnessed change can often carry forward into the next few years. And then to assess this, applying a series of different lenses, such as the potential for large business effects and the impact external forces may have. These we are going to call *the macro forces of change*.

Finally, it is also really important to sense check the predictions with area experts—seeking out the most cynically minded as they often, but not exclusively, can offer the sharpest refinement. And the predictions really do need to be sharp and defined otherwise they offer little utility, as they must also feel real world. To the point that you could hire for any predicted marketing role *today*—albeit the revenue contribution may not completely cover the investment. As the American-Canadian fiction writer, William Gibson, succinctly put it: "The future is already here—it's just not evenly distributed."

So, it is difficult to do and can risk credibility (being seen as an indulgence). But it is an important capability every business needs to build. And one that can lead to dramatic growth, particularly in times of change. Organizations that take a longer-term view tend to accelerate ahead of their competitorsin a time of disruption.

Harvard Business Review carried out a study that showed businesses that took a long-term view accelerated 47 percent ahead of businesses that took a shorter-term view throughout the global financial crisis of 2008/9. The disruption caused by a pandemic-led recession is likely to be a lot greater than an economic-led one. Therefore the opportunity for acceleration is greater.

Grow the business, by hiring.

The people that work within marketing can evolve the capability simply by hiring. Although marketing technology is an increasingly important aspect, a significant part of the product offering is based on brainpower. Therefore, a future business model could be created simply through the hiring of new talent with new skill sets.

However, it is easy to make a business case to hire people for roles that are required, and/or where a client or Financial Director has already agreed to fund. It is much harder to make the business case to invest in hiring for roles that do not already exist and where there is no revenue to fund them in the immediate term.

And it is exactly this that presents the opportunity for marketing. To identify the capabilities that will contribute a positive return to the business ahead of the competitors. And then to build a business case for hiring. A business case built on a return on the investment happening over a mid- to long-term timescale. In most cases the revenue will follow the talent. It is a calculated risk, but the upside could be significant. Any organization that can successfully define the capabilities for the future and build them today will inevitably accelerate ahead of the others.

If any marketing organization were to hire today, for example, a social-commerce strategist without any role or income to justify investment it is highly likely that within 12 months that individual will be contributing and generating income to justify the salary cost. In the wider context of business investment, the investment in more advanced resource is a low-risk investment; and should be considered more regularly by organizations.

However, it should not be about randomly hiring different capabilities without a vision. It needs to start with a clear sense of the gaps today and the openings for tomorrow.■

Predicting the capabilities of the future■

To start to build for the future requires an understanding of how marketing roles are changing, so we can use the observable direction of travel to project forward.

To that end we carried out a quantitative studyamongst people working within marketing and marketing services, to identify how the type of work is changing to see if we can draw any insights.

This started with the categorization of the different types of functions carried out by people working within the broader field of marketing communications. A list of day-to-day functions was created, which we reduced to 35 roles (reducing any further lost some of the granularity in the roles). See overleaf a list of the different functions categorized by the *type* of function: Reporting, Analyzing, Planning, Originating, Producing and Executing.

The 35 Marketing Communication Functions

Reporting

Building/Updating/Maintaining a Reporting Dashboard

Compiling a Competitive Analysis

Digital Performance Reporting

Reporting Audience Insights

Analyzing

Any Form of Advanced Analytics (e.g. Consumer Journeys, Propensity Modeling

Carrying out Budget Setting Analysis with MMM Data

Carrying out Data Analytics (Analyzing and Building Audience Segments)

Consulting on and/or Running a Brand Tracking Study

Consulting on and/or Running an MMM (Market Mix Model

Consulting on and/or Running an MTA (Multi-touch Attribution)

Executing

Any Form of Media Negotiation and Buying (via Phone, Face to Face or Email)

Digital-Commerce Activation within Third-Party Platforms (e.g. Amazon)

Engaging, Assessing or Booking Production Company

Liaising with Media (to Generate PR)

Programmatic Buying within a Trading Platform (DSP or Search/Social Platform)

Originating

Creating Brand Platforms/Propositions (Internal Facing

Creating Campaign Ideas (Consumer Facing)

NB: We have attempted to capture all of the major functions; however we are aware there are likely to be some we have missed. And some of the functions have been captured crudely.

Producing

Managing DCO (Dynamic Creative Optimization) Activity

Micro-content Production (Multiple assets for Online/Social)

Producing Branded Content

Product/Service Development

Planning

Assessing and Building an Approach for Ad- or Marketing-technology (DSP, Ad-server, CRM, etc.)

Conceiving and Managing Brand Integrations

Inventory Curation (e.g. Creating Bespoke Inventory Lists)

Managing a DAM (Digital Asset Management)

Managing a Purpose/CSR Workstream

Overseeing Data Privacy/Compliance

Planning a Digital-Commerce Campaign

Planning a PR Campaign

Planning Search (PPC or SEO)

Social Media/Influencer Management

Sponsorship Strategy and Management (including Product Placement)

Training on Science-based Insights (Marketing-, Demand- or Behavioral-Science)

Website Analytics/Maintenance and Optimization

Writing a Campaign Strategy

The research included a survey of people working across all marketing services agencies, asking them to what extent do they carry out each function today, and how that compares with five years ago and 10 years ago. This provided a workable view on how the different functions have changed over time.

We then engaged WARC in order to conduct a global survey of marketers, surveying people that work within marketing roles across all organizations and people that work within agencies.

WARC and PHD Research | What does the future of marketing look like?

- Respondent: Marketing decision makers (minimum of 10 years experience)
- Sample size: 1,721
- Survey period: March 2021
- Markets:

NAM: US, Canada

APAC: Singapore, Hong Kong, China, Australia, New Zealand, India

EMEA: UK, Ireland, France, Germany, Spain, Italy, Sweden, Netherlands, Russia, UAE, South Africa, Nigeria

LATAM: Mexico, Colombia, Argentina

The first part of the research was to establish the degree to which each of the 35 functions are carried out regularly —for 10 years ago and then for today. The survey showed a dramatic 51 percent increase in the overall activity[1], indicating increasing requirement for marketers and agencies to contend with an extending set of capabilities.

However, it is when you get into the data itself things start to become really interesting. And perhaps, for some of us, a little depressing.

[1]The average percentage claiming to have carried out/carry out functions, within each function type, regularly—comparing today (82 percent) versus 10 years ago (54 percent). This serves as a good proxy for the extent of capabilities that need to be carried out by people within marketing and agencies.

Reporting has overtaken Origination as the most carried out function.

The largest function type has changed. Ten years ago, it was Originating. Today, confirming a lot of the industry's voiced concerns, it is Reporting. This suggests, in an oversimplistic way of course, that marketing communications today is firstly a reporting business before it is a creative business. Although Reporting is only marginally higher than Originating, it is the dramatic increase in prevalence of Reporting activities which many of us will feel keenly in the day-to-day reality of our roles.

Regularly Carry-out This Function (Type)

10 Years Ago			Today			%Ch
1	Originating	73%	1	Reporting	88%	57%
2	Reporting	56%	2	Originating	86%	18%
3	Producing	51%	3	Planning	83%	69%
4	Executing	50%	4	Producing	82%	61%
5	Planning	49%	5	Executing	81%	64%
6	Analyzing	46%	6	Analyzing	74%	62%
		54%			82%	

Source: WARC and PHD 2021
NB: All 35 functions grouped into one of six function types

However, there is more positive news. The largest change over the last 10 years has been in Planning activities —a 69 percent increase, moving up to third position in the rankings, which bears out the increasing levels of complexity, as covered in Chapter 1. Although interesting, this data does not necessarily provide us any direction for change. For that we needed to enquire about the future.

Looking ahead.

We then asked respondents to predict the regularity of carrying out these functions *10 years from now*. This will allow us to see the functions that may fall away, relative to the others, and those that will become more prevalent. Before we look at the functions individually, let's stay with the function *type*. The data suggests a further increase in overall activity, albeit not to the degree that we experienced in the last 10 years. However, we must not read too much into this, as there will be functions emerging that are not included in this list.

What is of more interest is that the data suggests that the marketing midlife crisis will lift—with creativity (Origination) returning to the top—with a predicted increase of six percent. It confirms what a lot of marketers have been saying publicly; focusing back on creativity as a way of driving brand growth.

Regularly Carry-out This Function (Type)

Today			**10 Years Time**			%Ch
1	Reporting	88%	1	Originating	91%	6%
2	Originating	86%	2	Reporting	90%	3%
3	Planning	83%	3	Producing	90%	10%
4	Producing	82%	4	Planning	89%	7%
5	Executing	81%	5	Analyzing	86%	16%
6	Analyzing	74%	6	Executing	83%	2%
		82%			88%	

Source: WARC and PHD 2021
NB: All 35 functions grouped into one of six function types

What can be pulled from the data with more confidence, is the predicted *change* in Analyzing functions, with a noticeable projected increase of 16 percent. This underscores the need to start investing ahead in bringing more analysts into the business.

What about individual functions?

The data becomes more revealing when you look at each of the individual 35 functions. This is particularly so when you overlay two more additional data points: the degree to which the function is fully resourced by the organization; and the degree to which the function has the potential to provide a large business impact.

See the chart showing the 35 functions ranked in order of the degree to which they are regularly carried out today across the entire global marketing communications industry. The arrow indicates the change that is expected over the next 10 years.

Function	Fully Resourced	Potential for High Business Impact (Revenue)
Creating Campaign Ideas (Consumer Facing)	93%	74%
Digital Performance Reporting	94%	65%
Writing a Campaign Strategy	96%	70%
Website Analytics/Maintenance & Optimization	95%	60%
Producing Audience Insights	94%	65%
Product /Service Development	89%	76%
Compiling a Competitive Analysis	93%	57%
Planning Search (PPC or SEO)	88%	50%
Producing Branded Content	91%	53%
Carrying out Data Analytics (Analyzing and Building Audience Segments)	92%	68%
Conceiving and Managing Brand Integrations	90%	56%
Overseeing Data Privacy/Compliance	86%	51%
Social Media/Influencer Management	89%	45%
Building/Updating/Maintaining a Reporting Dashboard	93%	57%
Planning a Digital-Commerce Campaign	88%	71%
Planning a PR Campaign	88%	57%
Any Form of Media Negotiation and Buying (via Phone, Face to Face or email)	88%	54%
Micro-content Production (Multiple assets for online/social)	89%	53%
Programmatic Buying within a Trading Platform (DSP or Search/Social Platform)	84%	49%
Consulting on and/or Running a Brand Tracking Study	84%	50%
Assessing and Building an Approach for Ad- or Marketing-technology	85%	62%
Sponsorship Strategy and Management (including Product Placement)	83%	46%
Liaising with Media (to Generate PR)	89%	49%
Creating Brand Platforms/Propositions (internal facing)	86%	55%
Digital-Commerce Activation within Third Party Platforms (e.g. Amazon)	81%	63%
Managing a Purpose/CSR Workstream	81%	43%
Engaging, Assessing or Booking Production Company	83%	40%
Any Form of Advanced Analytics (e.g. Consumer Journeys, Propensity Modeling)	84%	63%
Training on science-based insights (Marketing-, Demand- or Behavioral-Science)	82%	61%
Inventory Curation (e.g. Creating Bespoke Inventory Lists)	69%	37%
Managing a DAM (Digital Asset Management)	80%	43%
Consulting on and/or Running an MMM (Market Mix Model)	80%	56%
Carrying out Budget Setting Analysis with MMM Data	75%	54%
Managing DCO (Dynamic Creative Optimization) Activity	79%	44%
Consulting on and/or Running an MTA (Multi-touch Attribution)	74%	49%

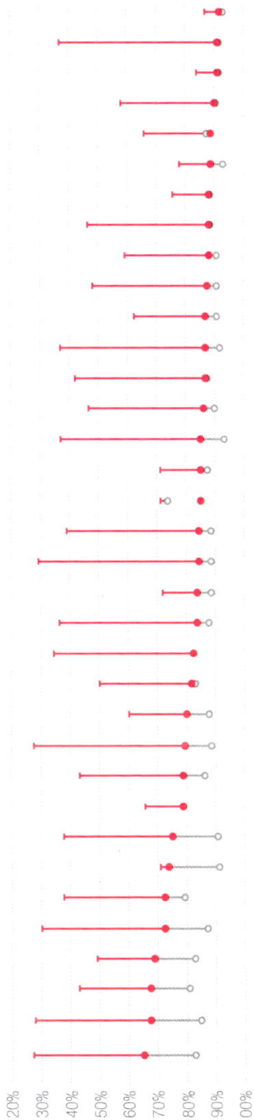

Key: Past (10 Years Ago) — Today — Future (in 10 Years)

The highest ranked functions should not be a surprise: creating campaign ideas, digital performance reporting and writing a campaign strategy. What is of interest is highly prevalent functions that are going to increase even further. These include: carrying out data analytics, conceiving and managing brand integrations, overseeing brand privacy/ compliance and planning a digital commerce campaign.

This indicates that the existing capability across these areas needs to be ready to start building additional resource. There needs to be an additional spotlight on overseeing brand privacy/compliance as according to the data this is under resourced, and digital commerce planning, which has a very high potential for business impact.

Perhaps even more revealing is some of the less prevalent functions today that are going to become highly prevalent (over 90 percent-plus regularly carried out in 10 years). These include any form of advanced analytics and training on science-based insights (marketing-, demand- or behavioral-science). These capabilities may need to be built into the organization, if they do not already exist.

As for overall potential for higher business impact the most important functions in order were: product/service development, creating campaign ideas and planning a digital commerce campaign. These are areas where the focus needs to be placed in order to advance the capability and to provide an incremental competitive advantage.

Combining the data in different ways to draw additional insight.

There are many ways to slice and dice the data to draw further revelations. For example, combining the unresourced percentage with the potential for high business impact in order to identify the functions that can deliver a lot, but are not properly invested in. These spotlight functions include digital-commerce activation within third-party platforms and assessing and building an approach for ad- or marketing-technology. These functions are most likely to not be fully resourced due to availability of talent, highlighting the importance to extend the filter from where organizations hire (as explored in Chapter 4).

We also combined the predicted future prevalence with the potential for higher business impact in order to identify the functions that are taking up a great deal of time and not necessarily contributing back to the business. The two functions that stood out on this measure were Managing a DAM (Digital Asset Management) and Managing a Purpose/CSR Workstream. The former is ripe for a significant advancement through the application of machine learning, which will be explored shortly. The latter is a more sensitive area and needs to be assessed through a marketing science lens in order to arrive at a more evolved perspective on its role within the wider business. Although this analysis is useful to confirm areas of focus for the future, it does not enable us to predict what new marketing roles will emerge. And that is what we are going to attempt to do next.

Predicting the new roles, that do not yet exist.

As well as identifying the roles that need investment today, we also need to attempt to project how these roles are going to evolve over time. From there we can start to plan for a different type of resource and also develop our existing resources in the direction of travel in which the function is heading.

Therefore, the final part of the study was to ask respondents to consider how the marketing functions could change in the future. To do that we had to *paint a picture* of the future, one that is both realistic and relevant to the day-to-day practical realities of marketing. We needed to understand the macro trends that are likely to impact marketing.

Defining the macro trends, relevant to marketing.

We approached Singularity University, a global learning and innovation community established by Peter Diamandis and Ray Kurzweil—with the help of Google's Larry Page—in 2008 at the NASA Research Park in California. Its brief was to help define the macro forces of change that are relevant to marketing.

In collaboration with Singularity University's Faculty and Innovation Strategist, Sally Dominguez, we defined six macro forces of change that are likely to impact marketing over the next five to 10 years: Physical Separation, Shallow Living, Trust Dissolution, Engineered Serendipity, Decentralized Influence and Purpose Pervasion.

Over the next two pages, you can take a detour and explore how these forces of change resulted in a reimagining of the important functions of the future.

The Six Macro Forces of Change | To 2030

(Relevant to Marketing)

1 **Physical Separation**

2 **Shallow Living**

3 **Trust Dissolution**

4 **Engineered Serendipity**

5 **Decentralized Influence**

6 **Purpose Pervasion**

NB: Developed in collaboration with Singularity University's Faculty and Innovation Strategist, Sally Dominguez, who focuses on exponential thinking, technology and trends for the future

1. Physical Separation

Spending more time connecting via screens

Post pandemic ramifications are likely to include a higher percentage of time spent working remotely, and interacting online with colleagues, customers and clients. Zoom, the most used virtual meeting app, increased usage 67 percent in Q1 of 2020 and was used by 90,000 schools in 20 countries: that number continues to increase. New employees may never meet their colleagues physically. Consumers will make purchases without touching the product or experiencing the brick and mortar store. This will have significant implications on the way that people live their lives, the way they interact with colleagues and the way they choose products.

Home workplaces, now frequented more often and seen online via virtual meeting spaces, become an extension of one's *personal brand*; if that even exists and whether we like it or not. Colleagues who have never physically met will see digitally altered images of their workmates and their surroundings. While the market for conferencing tools and new innovations to replace the current *online filters* will grow, this physical distance is likely to reduce the *connective-tissue* between employees and their companies—enabling people to be more portable (change jobs more easily and work across more than one company). We may also see an impact on the output in the form of lower levels of serendipity-led innovation, which tends to come less from structured brainstorms and more from unexpected connections and *off topic* impromptu discussions.

And there is the mental health issue also. Touch Starvation is a researched condition[4] that has been exacerbated by COVID. When people physically touch, our brains release oxytocin—a neuropeptide that increases happiness. Other mood-lifting chemicals include dopamine, serotonin and endorphins. Without these natural mood-enhancing chemicals people can experience depression, anxiety, stress and sleep disturbance.

 For sources please visit page 200

Organizations (that are trying to attract and retain the best talent) and brands (that are trying to attract and retain the most valuable customers) will need to adapt to a more *physically separated* landscape while ensuring the wellbeing of their stakeholders. The ones that do it best will grow ahead of their competitors.

2. Shallow Living

Increased multitasking leading to low levels of focus

People are so overwhelmed with stimuli across multiple devices that they do not engage properly and, instead, skim/scan/multiscreen/shallow process the world. The implication for marketers is significant. Online readers tend to read[5] around 50 percent of online content with 111 words or less, and their eyes follow an F or Z-pattern, drawn particularly to hyperlinks and bolded words. Research suggests[6] that online skim reading not only alters the reader's understanding of the text but may render them with less general understanding of the context, along with lower general levels of empathy, with implications for further increases in the rate of ad avoidance. Strategies for screen text would thus either adopt eye-catching patterns and short, simplified text or break the fourth wall and challenge the reader to dig deeper and thwart the urge to skim.

Video might appear the better digital alternative to text since videos are processed by the brain 60,000 times faster than text and have a higher share rate with viewers, but the way the brain digests videos is very different. Videos, for those that actually do watch them, are a form of passive viewing, whereas text requires active interest and brain activity to process words and ideas.

The power of this passive nature of video enables low interest information to be channeled into the brain, as it is not actively edited out as it would be when the person is in

For sources please visit page 200

an active processing mode. This partly explains the power of TV ROI. However, the major issue for marketers is that if the recent increase in time spent watching ad-free streaming services continues there will be a significant reduction in the opportunity for broadcast-level branding; reducing reach and inflating the cost.

Outside of video, marketers are going to have to work much harder to puncture the psyche, increasing the need for innovation.

3. Trust Dissolution

Increasing (at least 'claimed') distrust in organizations

At no time has trust been more tested or more valued. As of January 2021 a survey[7] of 33,000 people in 27 countries, found 57 percent believe government leaders, business chiefs and journalists are spreading falsehoods or exaggerations. Trust in the media, institutions, law enforcement and even science, is crumbling. The EY Future Consumer Index[8] has found that only 17 percent of consumers trust brands and only 16 percent trust media companies.

This is likely to have implications for marketing—at least for categories where trust plays an important role—with 88 percent of consumers claiming they demand trust when purchasing. Interestingly, regardless of how much consumers trust a brand, they still report[9] doing extensive research before purchasing. Even 75 percent of brand advocates report conducting substantial research prior to making the purchase. Therefore, trust and credibility will need to be constantly reinforced. And this is the case with data collection as well; with the demise of the third-party cookie, the focus turns squarely onto first party data. The collection of this data is, in part, dependent on trust.

However, it isn't just about avoiding low trust, there are likely to be benefits for achieving high(er) levels of trust. The

 For sources please visit page 200

2020 Edelman Trust Barometer[10] reports that 78 percent of consumers surveyed claimed they will advocate, recommend and defend a brand they trust. This is essential as algorithms increasingly assess user reviews in order to help us in suggesting, and soon deciding, on products or services.

The big question for marketers going forward, is how to build trust for their brands and to understand the direct and indirect ways that trust generates a positive contribution to revenue growth.

And, perhaps, the biggest issue with trust dissolution is in the area of data, with governments increasingly stepping in to regulate, placing further restrictions on the usage of data for marketing.

4. Engineered Serendipity

Ads predict and surface exactly what people want, next

Machine learning will increase in its predictive ability to surface up exactly what people are interested in before they even know it. An increase in the amount and type of *micro-reaction monitoring* data—such as the speed at which people scroll past a newsfeed post—will become the dominant fuel for predictive analytics.

The result: brand experiences that dynamically adapts to each person. Machine learning can create a more relevant brand experience, and in return consumers share their real time data. That is the value exchange. Considering the number of consumers shopping in micro moments (IBM/NRF reports[11] 71 percent of the 18,000 consumers surveyed globally) this ability to uber-personalize these 70-second moments could have a huge impact on sales.

Predictive analytics will not be restricted to screen monitoring only. It will increasingly use real-world data, beyond the standard location data currently available. This permissioned

For sources please visit page 200

mobile data will be mostly housed within the walled gardens of the major technology companies. With clean-room access to these data environments, marketers will be able to build predictive analytics, fueled by data on day-to-day behavior. One growth area is image recognition use: a 2020 Report[12] suggests 30 percent of internet users use image recognition tools already. Image recognition combined with real time personal data can greatly enhance useful choice management, particularly for those multi-tasking shoppers, and provide data for the algorithm.

And the resurgence of an old and previously dismissed digital-oddity—the QR code—created a role for itself in COVID-19. In 2020 11 million American households reported scanning a QR code[13], up from 9.7 million in 2018, and those statistics are pre-COVID-19 where bars and restaurants shifted their menus online; accessible with a quick scan of the QR using the phone's camera (a one click step). Of 2,062 US consumers surveyed[14] 72.1 percent are using their mobile phones in brick and mortar stores to access discounts, information and digital wallets via QR codes. Beyond the QR, a Mastercard survey[15] of 17,000 consumers in 19 countries worldwide found a 40 percent increase in contactless payments from January to April 2020 with 80 percent of those transactions under $25.

Not all of this data will be permissioned for use. But a lot will, enabling our online and offline lives to be engineered for serendipity. The implication for marketers, and their agencies, is to invest ahead of the competition in building an advanced predictive marketing capability, where an increasing number of marketing decisions are made by custom algorithms. These will be the new, highly protected, intellectual properties listed in the intangible-asset list on many major companies' balance sheets.

 For sources please visit page 200

5. Decentralized Influence

Everyone is an influencer

An increasing amount of media time is likely to shift from edited and curated media environments, such as linear TV stations and websites, to unedited and uncreated environments. This will take the form of multi screening and *multi-apping* across new platforms of text and video content populated with a range of interacting influencers. The foundations are already in place for this shift. A July 2020 Report[16] suggests more than half the world (3.96 billion) is now using social media and 3.91 billion via mobile phone, consuming 37 percent more media than their desktop-using counterparts. And people are increasingly using transient functions: disappearing content is rising, such as Instagram Stories and Twitter's Fleet tool, which can make content sharing harder to track for third-party apps[17].

However, to really see what this unedited and uncurated world could be like, peer over the shoulder of the online PC gamers with multiple screens and windows and a range of chat, video and live-cam views. Communicating brand messages in this environment is going to be a real challenge.

It also presents considerations for commerce. Direct selling—users selling direct to followers—continues to grow at over 10 percent, according to a pre-COVID survey[18]. Some early data showed[19] that micro-influencers with 10,000 or fewer followers, bring engagement and clicks for a low ROI. How to catalyze the marketing potential of these nano-influencers and even *normal* people with several thousand followers is already shaping up to be a major marketing battleground of the future.

For sources please visit page 200

6. Purpose Pervasion

Every brand is showcasing their purpose

In 2020, Deloitte[20] reported an "authentic purpose is now as important as *digital*." IBM and the National Retail Federation report[21] that over 70 percent of consumers are willing to pay up to 37 percent more for companies offering full transparency and traceability in their purpose and operations.

Irrespective of whether or not purpose-based *ad-campaigns* are a commercially viable route for marketing investment, people, when asked, *claim* purpose is important. This is a global consumer trend: A survey[22] of 8,000 respondents—covering Brazil, Canada, China, France, Germany, India, the UK and the US—revealed that 55 percent of respondents believe brands can more effectively solve social issues than governments, and 86 percent expect brands to solve societal as well as personal issues.

People also claim that *purpose* would encourage a change in brand preference—66 percent of US consumers[23] say they would switch from a brand they typically buy to a new product from a purpose-driven company, and would be willing to share that company's content on their social networks. And 72 percent of Gen Z[24] claims they are more likely to buy from a company that contributes to social causes.

Inevitably this data will lead to more purpose-based businesses. It will also lead to an increase in post-rationalized purpose-based ad campaigns which people will increasingly become wise to—60 percent of respondents reported *trust-washing* from brands in the last three years.

More worryingly, pervasive *purpose-pushing* will create a form of white noise, making it even harder to be heard, and frustrating organizations that are genuine in their efforts.

The concern for marketers, and their agencies, will be managing the communication of purpose as well as determining the new metrics for isolating and assessing the financial contribution of purpose-based investments.

 For sources please visit page 200

Smashing the functions against the forces.

As part of the survey, respondents were asked to consider how the functions they are more likely to be familiar with (that their organizations carry out) could evolve with the forces of change; selecting a force of change they believed would be an important factor in the future. So, respondents were only asked about what they understood and what they believed would happen. This was important in order to try, as much as we could, to increase the level of accuracy of prediction.

A small working team of strategists synthesized the results into the new marketing functions of the future. They had to be specific and real world. The functions were then sense checked against experts in the relevant fields.

Many of these functions have some form of existence today, albeit embryonic and/or confined to specialist agencies. *From our previous experience we have found that any prediction that does not have some form of existence at the time of prediction is most often wrong.*

The result of this is 15 new roles and/or capabilities. They are clustered into three groups, based on the function type: Originating–Producing, Planning–Executing and Analyzing–Executing. With Reporting being a requirement across all of them.

Many of these new roles could be hired by any marketing organization or agency *today*, and would be able to start to generate incremental return within the next 12 to 18 months. Some of them will require development to third-party technology-platforms, which will take a few more years. Above each one we have indicated the macro force of change and the function from which it was derived.

The 15 New Marketing Roles & Capabilities | Towards 2030

Originating–Producing Roles

[Macro Force: Engineered Serendipity] // [Function: Micro-content Production (Multiple assets for Online/Social)]

ML Creative Producer

Working within creative production software[1], which automatically creates multivariant ads across a range of ad-templates, dramatically reducing production time. With each ad showing a predictive performance score[2]. The team applies oversight and common sense, to the suggested multivariate ads, removing and adding elements with the predictive performance score adjusting as they make the changes. Leveraging insights from wider discipline such as marketing- and behavioral-science. Also including automated transcreation—auto-changing messaging for different languages/cultures[3].

1. *A further developed functionality than that which currently exists within existing platforms such as Adobe and Google and agency/consultancy specific platforms such as Adzu and Orca. Creative teams upload static fixed ads into the platform—the platform uses machine learning to turn them into templates and suggests a carousel of multiple related assets that could be used to create multi-variant versions covering an extended range of different templates, across all Display, Social, Video, Commerce, etc. Significantly reducing the time, and therefore cost, barrier that currently exists. With inbuilt, or connected to, DCO (Dynamic Creative Optimization) technology, enabling creative production and programmatic optimization to be linked.*

2. *Predictive scoring generated through using machine learning to auto tag creative, generating a significant data layer that can then be mined for performance: structured data (ad format, date, audience, context, etc.) and unstructured data (image within ads, semantic nature of headline, etc.). Likely to start with lower funnel metrics but over time will need to factor in the indirect and long-term contribution.*
3. *Will require specialist transcreation creative team in order to oversee. And also make strategic suggestions on communication specific to cultural holidays.*

[Macro Force: Decentralized Influence] // [Function: Writing a Campaign Strategy Recommendation]

Creator Collaborators[1]

Work with a portfolio of social influences (creators) that have been contracted to promote the brand, in order to help them exploit an increasingly advanced range of communication and commerce technologies emerging across social- content- and messenger-platforms. An important part of this will be managing the production, marketing and commerce component of live broadcasts[2/3].

1. *Already exists as a capability carried out by companies such as Viral Nation; mentioned here as likely to grow into a significant marketing function. Also, it is likely that the current specialists will take the position as being supply side (representing the best interests of the influencers) with a client-side function needing to be created within agencies.*

2. *Retailers such as Morphe cosmetics are turning retail into in-store studios. Offering professional lighting and film equipment, the spaces will increasingly be booked for Influencer broadcasts. Retail experience will be a hybrid between a shop and a live studio—some people working within retail will be mini/micro celebrities to very defined audiences.*
3. *Streaming will be steered based on a live data-feed on engagement.*

[Macro Force: Shallow Living] // [Function: Planning a Digital-Commerce Campaign]

Conversational AI Developers

Bringing together different technologies[1] in order to create interruptible ads; enabling people to interrupt the narrative flow of an ad and speak directly to one of the characters asking questions about the product/service and completing a purchase. *Until a technology company creates a self-serve platform to enable this, a range of support roles will be needed, bringing together all of the product/service information into one interrogatable cloud-based environment, integrating a chat-bot technology and designing the UX experience.*

1. *Such as Synthesia or Instreamatic for AI generated avatars and companies such as Teads to build the ad-unit which houses the content. PHD Global Business has identified and documented over 50 technology companies that offer capabilities required to create conversational AI.*

Planning–Executing Roles

[Macro Force: Various] // [Function: Various]

Consulting-Advisory

A diverse range of strategy and creative consultants and/or advisors[1]. Developing a range of off-the-shelf consulting products[2]. Of particular importance for clients that have in-housed the executional function. *Although consultancy has been in existence for a long time, it has remained small. However, with the increasing levels of complexity and an increase in clients in-housing executional functions, the requirement for this is likely to increase.*

1. *These individuals may be full-time employees of the agency and/or freelancers -- see 'Distributed Talent Management'*
2. *Important products will include Purpose-based Consultancy (from organizational change to marketing and assessing impact), Investment Planning (full-spectrum zero-based budgeting and allocation that looks across all areas, such as, retail media investments alongside paid media, and risk management) and Commerce Strategy (Including experts that are able to interpret the data and draw out genuine insights and the connected commercial implications/opportunities—this role will be more important than day-to-day data analytics which will ultimately be carried out by machine learning platforms such as Power BI by Microsoft—that uses natural language processing enabling people to ask questions of the data as opposed to having to do the analytics themselves).*

[Macro Force: Engineered Serendipity] // [Managing DCO (Dynamic Creative Optimization) Activity]

Technology Orchestration

A capability that links offsite, onsite and CRM activity together into one connected ecosystem[1]. Putting in place the infrastructure that enables the Decision Scientists to function. Requires highly technical capability to build interoperability between different technologies. And the management of ID graphs. Also requiring strong political[2] skills to bring together multiple stakeholders across different departments.

1. *Creating a closed-loop environment. Something that some consultancies, agencies and marketing organizations claim they have already achieved but few actually have. The technological barriers are significant, but will be overcome as the upside is great.*
2. *This capability needs to be built on both sides. A client-side capability that is anchored more in organizational change and a consultancy/agency side capability that has the ability to bring in technical expertise and connections with external technology companies.*

[Macro Force: Trust Dissolution] // [Function: Any Form of Advanced Analytics (e.g. Consumer Journeys, Propensity Modeling)]

Tech Company@Media Agency

An evolution of the current state of platform-certified individuals that already exist within agencies, to that of *entire platform teams that exclusively operate within the technology of the major tech companies*—for example, the teams at

Amazon, Google and Facebook[1]. With technologists, data scientists and analysts. The teams will be vendor-approved resellers of the technology platform and have deep links into the developers within each of the environments[2]. Enabling the agencies' clients to have first mover advantage on new technologies. Some will also develop an ISV (Independent Software Vendor) capability, developing software within the technology company cloud environments.

1. *Although some specialist agencies have already developed this, it hasn't fully developed as a capability within major agencies. Over time this may also include marketing technology companies such as Salesforce and SAP.*

2. *Agencies are likely to create bespoke applications that sit on top in order to solve for individual client requirements.*

[Macro Force: Physical Separation] // [Function: Digital-Commerce Activation within Third-Party Platforms]

Game Commerce

With more time spent gaming, a new capability to build a commerce layer within the major online gaming platforms[1]. Creating virtual products related to existing products in the form of branded skins, branded skills, including management of new forms of purchase/vendorship such as crypto currency and NFTs[2]. And a more significant development to include the management of all forms of eCommerce[3]—as gamers begin to purchase all categories but from within gaming platforms[4].

1. *Three types of video game platforms: Distribution/ Download (e.g. Steam), Live Streaming (e.g. Twitch) and*

Social (e.g. Discord). Twitch, owned by Amazon, is most likely to extend into wider ecommerce.

2. *A non-fungible token (NFT) is a unit of data stored on a digital ledger, called a blockchain, that certifies a digital asset to be unique and therefore not interchangeable. NFTs can be used to represent items such as photos, videos, audio and other types of digital files.*
3. *Subject to platform development, but possible advancement that will enable additional revenue to be generated.*
4. *This can extend beyond the gaming environments with partner endorsed merchandise, hard and soft bundles that can be bought in-app, in-game.*

[Macro Force: Engineered Serendipity] // [Function: Planning a Digital-Commerce Campaign]

Video Commerce

A deep understanding of, and a connection into, the different video environments[1] that enable viewers to tap to purchase any item featured—the car, the coat, the hotel. *Video Commerce is likely to take the form of different sub-specialisms such as those that work to get products featured within video (commerce-driven product placement), those that then set-up the products within the different platforms (as in the product information and, for some platforms, the connection to the brand's transaction engine). And then with a separate team that oversees the programmatic bid within the emerging software platforms.*

1. *Many media and technology companies are trialing and/or launching products: YouTube, NBC Universal, Dropp, with computer vision used to identify products automatically. Including specialist technology providers that work with existing platforms such as Seenthis, pioneering one-click shoppable formats.*

[Macro Force: Decentralized Influence] // [Function: Programmatic Buying within a Trading Platform (DSP or Search/Social Platform]

Influencer Programmatic Teams

Trading within influencer-programmatic platforms[1] that bid for mentions from social influencers; setting bid-factors based on type and length of mention[2]. *The supply-side side of this has already taken the form of self-serve platforms for influencers to identify brands they would like to promote and generate revenue from. Accessed directly by the influencers/creators and/or managed by the creator collaborators as a managed service.*

1. *With the rise of influencers and the increasing dominance of social commerce, technology platforms that link to advertiser-demand and influence-supply will grow. Existing platforms, such as Indahash, Buzzoole and Talify, and/or new platforms—yet to be created—will develop into the major trading platforms. With influencers managed as if media vendors, with private market place curation.*
2. *Optimized on a cost per conversion.*

Analyzing–Executing Roles

[Macro Force: Engineered Serendipity] // [Function: Carrying out Data Analytics (Analyzing and Building Audience Segments)]

Decision Science

Data scientists that train machine learning algorithms to make marketing decisions. Dynamically scoring privacy compliant user IDs or cohorts on purchase-propensity—constantly changing with their online behavior—connecting into the DSP as a bid factor[1]. Trained to make 50,000 bid-decisions a second[2] and then making a decision on the asset[3] to show. A capability that has been in development for a number of years, albeit fledgling. This more advanced capability will work within the environment that is created by the Technology Orchestration team, enabling the connection offsite, on site and CRM into one closed-loop, self-optimizing, environment, and incorporate LTV (lifetime value)[4]. *Connected to this will be the valuation of the proprietary algorithms, listed as intangible assets on the balance sheet.*

1. *In a post third-party cookie world, an important part of this is likely to include the management of a unified ID solution, working with first party data sets in a privacy compliant way; or accepting the trade-offs that come from having to work with cohorts, not individuals.*
2. *A crude approximation of the number of advertising impressions in a typical developed market for every second. For each one the algorithm will decide the value of the impression, setting the bid factor.*
3. *A combination of components within an ad unit or web/app environment. With the ability to carry out auto adjusting the language of the ad to suit the language of individual.*

4. *With the possibility of additional metrics in the form of environmental impact, enabling marketing to report back to the board on their contribution to the sustainability agenda.*

[Macro Force: Trust Dissolution] // [Function: Assessing and Building an Approach for Ad- or Marketing-technology]

Cleanroom Development Teams

Teams that work with third-party businesses[1] in order to provide access to their data within their own cloud environment[2]. Enabling external access to their data, in a compliant way. Connecting to an SSP/DSP—and commerce platforms—in order to execute against first party data and measure the resultant impact on sales. *Once established, the Decision Science team will build proprietary algorithms to optimise[3].*

1. *The priority will be major retailers, where there is a lot of transaction data. However, this would extend to a wider range of businesses. It is also likely to be used for rights vendors that have developed a fan base—adding an additional revenue stream within the traditional sponsorship model—with rights holders considering the fan in much the same way as Amazon considers the customer and enabling third-party companies to sell direct to them.*

2. *Specialist technology companies will develop platforms to encourage third-party companies to create clean room environments. However, large holding companies have relationships with major technology companies and therefore can offer incentivization and support.*

3. *Developing new measurement analytical products such as a cross walled garden approach to MTA.*

[Macro Force: Trust Dissolution] // [Function: Carrying out Data Analytics (Analyzing and Building Audience Segments)]

Publisher-Audience Management

Working with online publishers to build *online publisher* cloud environments, which are linked to a SSP and/or a DSPs[1]. This will enable privacy-compliant analysis and targeting of first-party data *across the open-web*. Important for targeting attribute-based audiences[2]. *Publishers may, in effect, becoming mini technology platforms.*

1. *Online publishers will see the value in their own first party data increase with the depreciation of the third-party cookie. With this they are likely to set-up clean room environments with linked SSP/DSPs, onboarding agencies/clients and/or provide a manage service. The value of publisher first party data will be for audiences that are not successfully expanded through the lookalike modeling approach, such as Google's FLoC, and where the wastage from the extended size does not justify the data costs. In some markets, neutral parties, e.g. the IAB, may successfully encourage publishers to house their first party data within a central privacy safe environment that all advertisers then work within. Importing their own first party data in order to create a unified ID solution*

2. *Google's cohort algorithm is likely to be highly effective for interest-based audiences, such as people interested in healthy eating. Where it may struggle is in attribute-based audiences, for example, people with gluten intolerance. For attribute-based audiences focusing purely on addressable first party IDs is the only way that the cost of the data will be justified. And this is the unique advantage that publishers, and third-party businesses/ organizations, have.*

Other Supporting Roles

[Macro Force: Various] // [Function: Various]

AaaP (Agency as a Platform)

Management, strategy, contractual, recruitment[1], training and technical support for clients that in-house executional functions. With a range of clearly scoped-out services that the client organization can pull into their business. For media agencies, specifically, this will also include technology provision in the form of planning and reporting software, access to third-party preferential rates, specialist expertise and the curation and management of inventory.

1. *The hiring and replenishment of talent will be an important function. Particularly as the roles of marketing become more specialized and finding talent becomes harder. Some agencies will, in effect, become quasi-recruitment companies.*

[Macro Force: Physical Separation] // [Function: Various]

Distributed Talent Management

The collation and management of a distributed workforce of consultants and freelancers. Will require an understanding of the different areas of marketing communications and how they are evolving[1]. Will be able to bring in the right expertise directly into projects in order to enhance the capability. *Over time this role will develop into ways of keeping the distributed workforce connected and engaged; this may also include how they connect into the employees within the organization. Workflow and collaboration software are likely to be playing an important part. Perhaps with lightweight gamified layer to keep people highly engaged.*

1. *This role may sit within an agency and/or spawn into a separate specialist agency.*

[Macro Force: Trust Dissolution] // [Function: Carrying out Data Analytics (Analyzing and Building Audience Segments)]

Data Consultancy

Consultancy on the management of first party data, as the techniques for usage evolve[1],with the development of clean rooms, unifying of IDs, cohort structures, commerce and predictive analytics, the requirements for consent change. Although the discipline exists, it is mostly a regulatory activity and not a fully developed consultancy practice[2].

1. *As marketers become more sophisticated with the usage of data they will constantly need a team of privacy consultants to make sure that the data usage is compliant, and also retrospectively changing the consumer-consent so that it is always up-to-date with the changing nature of how the data is being used.*
2. *Law firms do not necessarily have the required technical understanding of how marketers use the data across a range of technology platforms.*

Beyond the five- to 10-year horizon.

There are a range of more hyperbolic-sounding roles which are often cited in these types of predictions that *may start* to emerge towards the end, and just after, the five- to 10-year window. These are hard to predict as they are dependent on development of new consumer technologies that do not yet exist; these roles include: Layer Designers (developers that create entertainment, commerce and utility information that is superimposed on the world via mixed reality headsets); VR World Designers (developers of virtual experiences for brands); and BCI (Brain Computer Interface) Developers (working with companies such as Elon Musk's Neuralink to create *appropriate* brand funded utilities).

And some roles will only develop after the predicted 15 new roles have fully developed. For example, advances in quantum computing could allow predictive analytics to evolve into simulation development of the entire client marketplace. Currently, such an endeavor is mathematically chaotic in nature—running models across every conceivable combination of actions is highly susceptible to small changes in the initial setup—and optimization is impossible. It is already suspected that quantum computing represents a probabilistic solve for such challenges and the 2040s could see Quantum Simulation Developers simulating the entire media universe for a client.

From in-housing to in-platforming, another thing for agencies to think about.

Some agencies have been working with their clients on their in-housing agenda. The additional area of consideration for agencies is now coming from a different direction. Technology companies in-housing, or perhaps more appropriately termed *in-platforming*, a range of functions that are typically carried out by the agency. Over the next five to 10 years we are likely to see them develop a range of services that feel very much like an agency. Either to agencies as an extended capability or offered directly to clients. The consideration for marketers, of course, is the degree to which the external support is tied to a particular platform/solution. Although this is a recognized factor for areas such as selecting a financial adviser (where it is clear that the financial advisor is either tied or independent) it has not factored as much as it should for the procurement of marketing services.

Organizing this new heterogeneous talent base of the future is the final consideration of *Shift*. In Chapter 3 we explored where certain roles should sit based on the characteristic of the company. In Chapter 4 we explored the future model of work of a decentralized network of experts.

This new talent base will sit across agency, marketing organization and within specialist service businesses, which will also include the management and provision of freelancers.

With the increasing level of specialism will come an increasing array of different functions. This is likely to place a commercially unsustainable burden on the marketing organization in order to keep pace as most organizations will not be able to afford to fund all of the different specialist expertise they will need (or, at least, will not be able to fund 100 percent of an individual when they only require 20 percent). There will become an increasing reliance on the agency, which will be able to fund each of the emerging functions as the cost will be shared by a range of clients. This is also the case for any marketing organization that has in-housed activation functions. They will also benefit from having advanced services wrapped around them in order to develop existing employees and provide stretch- and overflow-capability.

A blurring of the boundaries.

An increasing amount of the consultancy and executional functions provided by external agencies are likely to be embedded into the client organization—operating seamlessly as part of the *client* teams as opposed to being a fixed and separate agency offering, mediated through an account director. This is already starting to happen according to Unilever's Conny Braams: "These changes in the wider ecosystem of brands have opened up many new opportunities and responsibilities which have led to new ways of working with our partners."

> ***"These changes in the wider ecosystem of brands have opened up many new opportunities and responsibilities which have led to new ways of working with our partners."***
>
> *Conny Braams*
> *Chief Digital and Marketing Officer at Unilever*

Furthermore, existing and new technology will be used to connect everyone, irrespective of where they sit, with agency platforms connected to client-based platforms to enable sharing of data. We are already seeing this happening across the business. And with this the client and the agency become more interconnected. A view reinforced by Isabel Massey, Global Head of Media at Diageo, when reflecting on the key priorities underpinning their global media review in 2019: "When we underwent our global media agency review, our expectations were summed up by our ask for: a borderless partnership grounded in expertise, radical candor, radical transparency and the utmost respect for the people we market to."

"A borderless partnership grounded in expertise."

Isabel Massey
Global Head of Media at Diageo

And as well as borderless, the new relationships need to be designed to be agile and flexible, so that they can adapt and change to the requirements of the market. Massey added: "It would be a mistake to build a marketing model that works for 'now', rather than building a model that is agile and flexible to meet evolving needs."

According to David Indo, Founder of ID Comms, this phenomenon has already started and will take hold as we progress towards 2030, changing the nature of the relationship between the client and the agency. "We won't be seeing pitches as regularly as we do currently, and price will be an incidental component of media reviews. I think we'll begin the formative years of a long, long chapter where brands and their agency partners will form deep strategic relationships, where you won't need to pitch every three to five years because there simply won't be the commercial rewards. You'll course correct, but you'll stay with your agency partner—unless there is something fundamentally troubling—for decades, because they will become fiber-entwining partnerships of the future."

If this is the case marketing organizations are going to have to rethink on how to assess their external partners.

New KPIs needed.

If marketers are going to keep the same agency for many years, they will need to develop new ways of making sure their contribution is at a consistently high level. A greater understanding of the contribution the agency is offering the business is going to be essential. And agencies, in part pressurized by the *client*, are likely to compartmentalize the marketing services they provide so they can each be assessed on their contribution: *What's the revenue contribution the commerce team is adding?* What about the social influencer team? This will enable the *core* agency support function to represent the client's best interest.

As a parallel, the relationship between marketers and the outsourced experts may start to resemble the relationship people have with wealth managers, where the level of complexity is beyond that which most clients can, or have time to, understand. And therefore, are less able to direct and approve multiple decisions. For example, deciding on a specific curated set of inventory, and amalgamation of first party data sets and/or a new proprietary algorithm. Or deciding on multivariate, multi-template strand of creative work. In this new world marketers need to fully make the move from inputs to outputs.

From inputs to outputs.

This could lead to a change in the very nature of how marketers engage external support. Instead of focusing on the individual decisions that have been made by the outsourced partner, the focus is on the output, as in the impact on the business. How the outsourced group of experts, perhaps consolidated into agency or sub agency groups, achieve the business result is, to some extent, up to them. In this situation the client simply judges them, like individuals judge their investment manager, on results.

Andrew Robertson, BBDO Worldwide, said: "There are two preconditions for an effective agile working model. First, you must have the metric that matters. Whilst that's easy if you are selling direct, asking people to download apps or operating in what is called the *performance* space, it is less frequently defined for demand generating, brand building activity. But it's not beyond the wit of agencies and clients to solve this. The second is much tougher. In a truly agile model a small multifunctional team is empowered to iterate and ship to drive up this metric, based on outcomes. The reality of the culture and operating systems of most clients, and as a consequence agency teams, is that they are driven by approvals, not outcomes.

"We have people who require the approval of ideas that are being designed to secure the approval of others. Once we get the final approval, we all say: 'ok now let's see what happens?'. An inordinate amount of time and resource goes in to getting approvals, on both sides. If we could focus on optimizing against outcomes rather than approvals, we could have a relationship more like a wealth manager, for example, 'invest this money and tell me how we're doing'."

Whilst this is accepted practice in the performance space, it has not, in any meaningful way, expanded into mid and top funnel marketing investments. One of the reasons for this, beyond the culture of approvals, is the issue of measurement. According to Robertson it is simply down to the fact that "we don't have the metric that matters, that we should be optimizing against—even though this is not difficult to solve."

As mentioned earlier, any prediction that is likely to happen will often have an existence in the present. This outcome-based approach has been used by digital and mainstream media agencies for performance-based marketing, with some major clients building it into their contracts. However, creating an early indicator metric that incorporates the *indirect* and *long-term* contribution that comes from a broad scope of marketing activity is still, for many clients and agencies, not defined.

Recent work into the predictive power of search for future market share shifts has been explored by Les Binet of adam&eveDDB. This sort of analysis, with a bit of machine learning thrown in to account for all of the other variables that impact the business, may offer the potential for a predictive KPI that could enable a shift towards outcomes and, therefore, rethinking of the client agency relationship.

What is certain is that the client and agency combination that crack this first is likely to accelerate ahead of the competitive set. As every single moment and every single action of every single person will single-mindedly be focused on the ultimate KPI■

Final reflections on the future■

The roles set out in this chapter and the new ways of organizing them are, to some degree, available for marketers today. It is likely that the investment in this new talent will not pay back immediately. But building it in now will ultimately enable the organization to get ahead of change. This is the most dramatic impact we, as an industry, can make to bring the future into the present more quickly: to evolve the capability simply by hiring.

Although harder to make the business case to invest in hiring for roles that do not already exist, this is the opportunity for marketing. A business case built on a return on the investment happening over a mid- to long-term timescale.

In most cases the revenue will follow the talent.

And then to consider how best to build this new capability into the existing structures. With new KPIs that can enable a more agile approach. Where the focus is on outputs. And where everyone is aligned.

Any organization that can define the capabilities for the future and build them today will inevitably accelerate ahead of the others.

But it is not easy. But that is what true leadership should do. To see something that others cannot see. And align people to that vision.

And shift the organization in that direction■

Summary

Summary

In summary:
The key things to remember from *Shift*.

Let's take a moment to pause. And reflect on where we have just been. After a very long decade and the resultant *Cambrian explosion* of new features, the marketing industry changed dramatically.

To start with it was all so exciting, with brand-new marketing and media channels and activities opening up for the first time. But it was also the Wild West, leading to the necessary creation of new ad-technologies to manage such things as bot-traffic and inclusion and exclusion lists.

And with the dramatic increase in media spend into the major digital media vendors, we witnessed their inevitable rise into the oligopolies of today. This, combined with the hypnotizing effect of new data and accurate forms of measurability, reshaped the marketing agenda.

A consequence of this was digital transformations for many companies. But it also led to an over focus on short-termism. Which, towards the end of the long decade, had an observable impact on the overall potential for marketing to affect a business.

Digitalization of the marketing agenda was also having another impact. Not on the balance sheet but on the minds of the people that worked in marketing, creating anxiety for people not to feel like they are dinosaurs. And that they are part of the new world.

This all led to the marketing midlife crisis of today. With many organizations displaying one of a range of different midlife crisis typologies, from *The Madonna*, where the obsession is on constant reinvention, through to *The Harry Houdini* where an over focus, and sometimes overinvestment, is made in technology to magic a way forward.

The way through is to focus on the individual. To remove ambiguity in order to allow a greater level of clarity on one's own contribution to the organization. Enabling people to focus their minds on the business—instead of the creation of positive perceptions on how well they are doing. And for the leaders of the business to be super clear on what the company's reason for existing is, beyond money. Creating a galvanizing and motivating driver for all that enter the business.

And then going further, to start to build a healthier functioning ecosystem. Where greater clarity and simplicity is placed on the capabilities that are required and where they best sit. Using a framework of how centralized the client organization is and the degree to which it is marketing or product focused in order to define the capabilities required and where they should be housed.

And connected to this, a greater clarity on which roles should be in-housed; with a minimum requirement of the core leadership functions across the broad range of marketing disciplines of today. Allowing enough bandwidth for the increasingly specialist agency services to communicate fully with the business.

For some marketers that do want to go further and in-house practitioner and execution capabilities, the agencies need to change the nature of their product. Providing platform-based services such as talent provision, training and replenishment. Overflow and advanced support. The negotiation of contracts. The provisioning of inventory. And technology.

In this new world a course correction is needed in our collective focus, to the most important part of the business: talent. The rebalancing of the agenda away from marketing technology back onto individuals is long overdue. This does not mean technology and data is not absolutely essential and pivotal to the modern marketing machine. It is simply that the agenda has moved too far away from talent. We need to apply the same level of advanced and precision thinking, that we have applied to data and technology over the last 10 years, to our people.

Taking inspiration from the *gurus* of personal development to help us explore how marketing organizations can evolve to become true people-centric organizations. And within this, a rethinking of our organization into learning institutions that happen to do business, for the ultimate objective of extracting the maximum contribution of our talent.

And a new look at our talent management through the lens of swim lanes. This is essential for a more heterogeneous future, one where many functions will be carried out by people that sit outside the organization.

Preparing for this new future with a systematic approach to prediction. Decomposing marketing services into 35 functions, and then using research in order to predict the ones that will be more important in the future. Those that will offer the greatest business impacts and are not yet fully resourced. Using the *six macro forces of change* in order to consider how these functions will evolve over time. Enabling us to attempt to predict the roles of the future, today.

And finally, considering how these new roles, and the functions they provide, will change the nature of the agency and client relationship. One that will become more entwined and embedded. And yet able for individual components to be assessed on their actual contribution. With compound KPIs that are early indicators of overall marketing impact on the business.

Allowing clients to have more support, but more control, to add and remove marketing-services based on the payback. Providing the same level of assessment that marketers currently have over the various media channels and assets that they deploy.

And, of course, the industry will continue to evolve. At some point we will all hand over the reins to the next generation. We must make sure that we pass it on intact. And that we can say that we moved it on. That we took the time to think long-term. To build the future.

This was the ambition of *Shift*. To help in that endeavor. We hope it has contributed in some way.■

The Six Macro Forces of Change | To 2030.

[4] https://onlinelibrary.wiley.com/doi/full/10.1111/jocn.15488

[5] https://www.nngroup.com/articles/how-little-do-users-read/

[6] http://www.cwu.edu/english/sites/cts.cwu.edu.english/files/documents/Encountering Empathy.pdf

[7] https://www.edelman.com/trust/2020-trust-barometer

[8] https://www.ey.com/en_us/future-consumer-index

[9] https://www.ibm.com/downloads/cas/EXK4XKX8

[10] https://www.edelman.com/trust/2020-trust-barometer

[11] https://www.ibm.com/thought-leadership/institute-business-value/report/consumer-2020

[12] https://datareportal.com/reports/digital-2020-july-global-statshot

[13] https://scanova.io/blog/qr-code-statistics/

[14] https://securecdn.pymnts.com/wp-content/uploads/2020/04/Remote-Payments-April-2020.pdf

[15] https://www.mastercard.com/news/press/press-releases/2020/april/mastercard-study-shows-consumers-globally-make-the-move-to-contactless-payments-for-everyday-purchases-seeking-touch-free-payment-experiences/

[16] https://datareportal.com/reports/digital-2020-july-global-statshot

[17] https://www.pcmag.com/news/social-privacy-is-on-the-rise-almost-half-of-social-media-accounts-are

[18] https://www.awin.com/us/market-insights/the-awin-report

[19] https://influencermarketinghub.com/influencer-marketing-2019-benchmark-report/

[20] https://www2.deloitte.com/global/en/pages/about-deloitte/articles/global-report-home.html

[21] https://www.ibm.com/downloads/cas/EXK4XKX8

[22] https://www.edelman.com/trust/2020-trust-barometer

[23] https://www.conecomm.com/research-blog/2018-purpose-study

[24] https://www.businesswire.com/news/home/20200706005543/en

More on the organizations of the contributors:

WARC is a global advertising research company, owned by Ascential, a specialist information, data and analytics company that helps the world's most ambitious businesses win in the digital economy.

The **Singularity University** (www.su.org) is a community of entrepreneurial leaders making a positive impact at planetary scale, helping our members harness the power of exponential technology to improve the lives of billions throughout the world. SU's community of more than 250,000 members is at the forefront of scientific, technical and economic innovation as part of SU's ecosystem, working on addressing humanity's most urgent challenges.

The Mini MBA in Marketing was founded by Mark Ritson. The MBA teaching has been recognized with teaching awards at LBS, MIT and MBS. Widely acknowledged as one of the world's leading marketing educators.

The **Ehrenberg-Bass Institute** is the world's largest center for research into marketing. Led by Professor Byron Sharp, Institute Director and author of *How Brands Grow—what marketers don't know,* the Ehrenberg-Bass team works with brands all over the world to help marketers develop and benefit from a culture of evidence-based marketing.

The **London School of Economics** (often referred to as LSE) is a public research university located in London, England.

PHD Frameworks

These are some of the frameworks that you might find useful when applying *Shift* to your organizational challenges.

Talent
Delusion
Innovative Thinking
Matrix
Empowering
Creative
Desired Outcome
Fluid
Energy and Passion
Innate Strengths
Where are we going?
Agile
Change Everything

The Five Marketing Midlife Crises Archetypes.

	The King Henry VIII	**The Madonna**
	CHANGE EVERYTHING	WHAT'S NEW?
PRIMARY CONDITION:	Dissatisfaction	Distraction
HOW TO SPOT IT:	Continual and abrupt changes to the agenda *(with implication for personnel and agencies)*	An overfocus on the next big thing *(at the expense of what drives the business, today)*
PRACTICAL SOLUTIONS:	Assessment of Best-in-class *(and skill gaps — to create a realistic point of comparison and perspective for change)*	Build measurement framework *(linking all marketing input to marketing output)*
DESIRED OUTCOME:	Everyone *informed* making fewer but better decisions	Everyone *focused* on activities that actually contribute

The Christopher Columbus	The Donald	The Harry Houdini
WHERE ARE WE GOING?	LISTEN TO ME	LOOK AT THIS!
Disarray	Delusion	Denial
Little/no understanding on where the business is heading *(and the role for marketing)*	Unsupported and unevidenced dogma on how marketing works	Confounding with complexity and 'magic-solutions' *(that do not have claimed impact)*
Create long-term vision *(with road-map and how marketing contributes to this)*	Investment in learning *(into marketing science—starting with leaders first)*	Institutionalize feedback *(so leaders can understand real world impact and/or employees are skilled)*
Everyone *clear* on the way forward	Everyone *enlightened* on how marketing works	Everyone *heard* and on the same page

Organizational Audit.

Unhealthy Organizations and Agencies:

Foundation	Assessment	Indicators
1. Technology	Inflexible	Outdated legacy technology that creates inefficiencies (and that is not 'interoperable'). 'Vendor-lock'—contracts with external technology providers that hold the company back.
2. Capability	Constrained	Employees deskilling as the practice of marketing communications becomes more advanced. A lack of funding for external marketing expertise.
3. Process	Cumbersome	Outdated processes kept in place to protect jobs. Processes to solve for a poorly structured organization.

Foundation	Assessment	Indicators
4. Insight	Narrow	Data is limited to PowerPoint charts. Data that is not impacting optimization and measurement.
5. Measurement	Limiting	Focusing on KPIs that are not linked to growth (for example, ROI). Different departments focusing on competing KPIs (brand vs. short-term).

Organizational Audit.

Healthy Organizations and Agencies.

Foundation	Assessment	Indicators
1. Technology	Empowering	Marketing and advertising technology platforms that free people up, giving them more time back for thinking. Inspire people with information and guidance to help them perform at a higher level.
2. Capability	Regenerative	Highly curious organizations that focus a lot on upscaling their workforce in the evolving areas of marketing communications. Bringing in new expertise to keep advancing the capability.
3. Process	Agile	Processes that empower people to make decisions (reduced lines of command). Technology platforms improve speed and foster collaboration.

Foundation	Assessment	Indicators
4. Insight	Vivid	Putting in place the right resource to draw commercial value from data. Partner with external services that can offer more advanced (for example, predictive) analytics.
5. Measurement	Fluid	Well understood KPI frameworks that link immediately to optimizable KPIs to business KPIs. Live reporting on overall business performance.

The Organizational Identity Matrix.

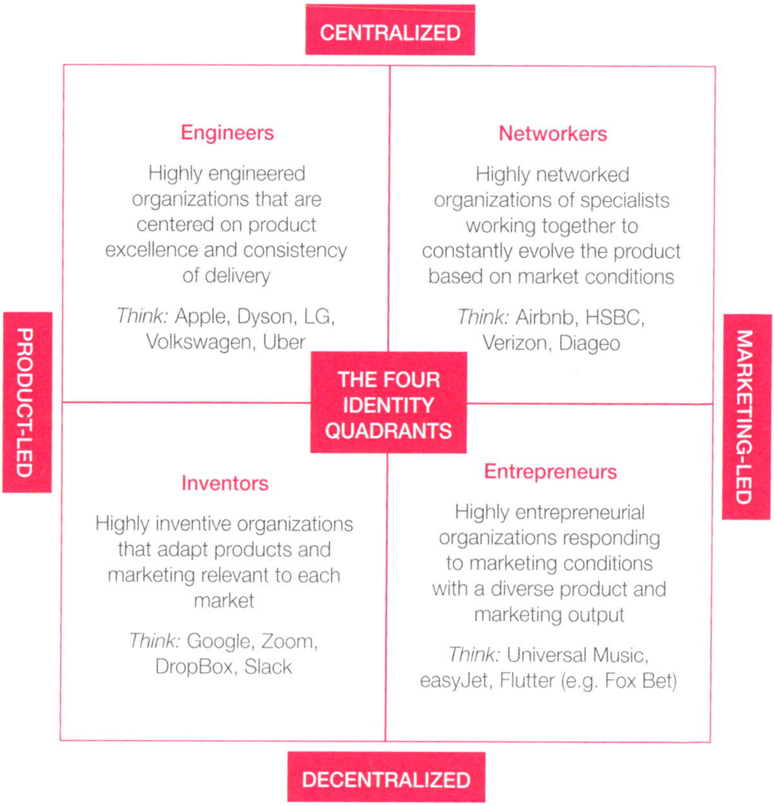

Challenger Types (Overthrow)
PHD and eatbigfish

What's your challenger type?

PEOPLE'S CHAMPION
A BRAND STANDING UP FOR A GROUP OF PEOPLE WHO HAVE BEEN SHORT-SERVED OR EXPLOITED BY THE ESTABLISHMENT FOR TOO LONG

ENLIGHTENED ZAGGER
THE ENLIGHTENED BRAND, DELIBERATELY SWIMMING AGAINST THE PREVAILING CULTURAL OR CATEGORY TIDE

IRREVERENT MAVERICK
POKE BEIGE IN THE EYE

DRAMATIC DISRUPTOR
A BRAND AND PRODUCT THAT DRAMATICALLY SIGNALS A REAL AND SIGNIFICANT PRODUCT OR SERVICE SUPERIORITY

NEXT GENERATION
THAT WAS THEN AND THIS IS NOW. NEW TIMES CALL FOR NEW PRODUCTS, SERVICES AND BRANDS

MISSIONARY
A CHALLENGER LOOKING TO CHANGE SOMETHING THAT IS WRONG OR UNFAIR IN THE WORLD AND WEARING THAT STRONG SENSE OF PURPOSE ON ITS SLEEVE

FEISTY UNDERDOG
STICK IT TO GOLIATH

LOCAL HERO
A CHALLENGER THAT CHAMPIONS THE IMPORTANCE AND CHARACTER OF LOCAL NEEDS, AS OPPOSED TO A GLOBAL MARKET LEADER

DEMOCRATISER
A CHALLENGER THAT TAKES SOMETHING PREVIOUSLY ONLY AVAILABLE TO THE FEW AND MAKES IT ACCESSIBLE TO THE MANY

REAL & HUMAN
A GROUP OF REAL PEOPLE WHO GENUINELY CARE ABOUT WHAT THEY'RE MAKING AND HOW THEY ARE SERVICING YOU

Innate Strengths:

TYPE	Strength	Roles
PRECISIONISTS	**Turns Disorder into Order** Able to learn new information quickly, are precise and detail oriented, have a strong adherence to rules, a drive for perfection, intellectual curiosity and are logical thinkers.	Analytical and highly technical roles
SOLUTIONISTS	**Finds a Way Through** Likely to be highly creative, exceptional problem solvers, original thinkers and talented visualisers. They are often exceptionally gifted verbally.	Creative and strategic development roles
RESILIANTS	**Pushes On** Likely to be highly resilient, tenacious, good at problem solving with strong verbal skills and empathetic strengths.	High-pressure roles, including client and stakeholder management
LATERALISTS	**Creates the Unexpected** Original thinkers, are creative, energetic and can have high levels of perseverance when interested in a topic. An ability to laser focus when engaged.	Creative and dynamic roles, where there is constant change
CONNECTORS	**Aligns Minds** Likely to have excellent listening skills, have great strengths in oral recall and memorization They can thrive in social communication.	Stakeholder-management and internal people development
DEVELOPERS	**Frames the View** Clarity of mind, able to construct and frame a perspective with clarity and order.	Strategic- and writing-based roles